Eritrea Sovereignty, a Struggle and Survival.

A State of Cultural diversity

Author
Marcel Mbarga

SONITTEC PUBLISHING. All rights reserved. No part of this publication may be reproduced, distributed, or transmitted in any form or by any means, including photocopying, recording, or other electronic or mechanical methods, without the prior written permission of the publisher, except in the case of brief quotations embodied in critical reviews and certain other noncommercial uses permitted by copyright law. For permission requests, write to the publisher, addressed "Attention: Permissions Coordinator," at the address below.

Copyright © 2019 Sonittec Publishing
All Rights Reserved

First Printed: 2019.

Publisher:
SONITTEC LTD
College House, 2nd Floor
17 King Edwards Road,
Ruislip
London
HA4 7AE

Table of Content

TABLE OF CONTENT **4**

ERITREA SOVEREIGNTY **1**

HISTORICAL VIEWPOINT **1**
EFFORTS EXERTED TO FIND PEACEFUL SOLUTION 11
ERITREA CONSTITUTIONAL GOVERNANCE **13**
INDEPENDENCE ERITREA [THE SILVER JUBILEE]! **19**
AN EXPENSE FOR LIFE OF ALL! **26**
FOREIGN POLITICAL AND DIPLOMATIC ACTIVITIES **34**
VALUATION OF EPLF'S FAMILIARITY IN THE PERIOD BETWEEN ITS 1ST AND 2ND CONGRESS **45**
EXPANSIONISM IN THE HORN **58**
POLITICAL AND MILITARY STRUGGLE, ANTI COLONIALISM **62**
FIRST PART 62
SECOND PART 66
THIRD PART 70
FOURTH PART 75
FIFTH PART 79
SIXTH PART 83
SEVENTH PART 87
EIGHTH PART 90
NINTH PART 94
TENTH PART 98
ELEVEN PART 102
STRATEGIC WITHDRAWAL AND THE SECOND CONGRESS OPTIONS FOR MILITARY DEVELOPMENT **105**
Military planning that out-maneuvered enemy military elites 116
The successive offensives and liberation of Eritrea 122
CULTURE **127**
Wedding Tradition 127

What Happens After the Wedding?	135
Romance Perspective	147
Culture driver for development	157
Eid Etiquettes	165
'Writing our history	173
Social Gathering	185
Homage to coffee: A colorful nature of Eritrean culture	194
Tour, See and Believe!	200

Eritrea Sovereignty

Historical Viewpoint

Early Development of the Eritrean Workers' Movement

Almost 80 years have elapsed since the Eritrean workers' movement began in the 1930s. The Eritrean workers' movement whose development was closely linked with the rapid Italian industrial colonial economy created in the country was one of the first workers movements, that is historically remembered for its advanced technical skills and high level of consciousness in the African continent at that time. When Eritrea established a federal system of government in 1952, the Confederation of Free Eritrean Labour Unions was a formally recognized member of the International Labour Organization (ILO) and had started to participate in its conferences. At that time the rest of African states were still under the yoke of the European colonialism. This legal status and freedom of the Eritrean workers was, however, curtailed by the intensive campaigns of terror that the Ethiopian regime of emperor Haileselassie unleashed, forcing the ranks and file of the Eritrean workers associations to be dispersed.

The historical development of the organization and movement of the Eritrean workers is directly related to the colonial challenges and experiences of the struggle waged to liberate the country from consecutive colonial powers. In the first phase during the Italian fascist colonial rule (1935-1941) the Eritrean workers' movements took simple forms that of opposing the severe racial discrimination and exploitation, improving their social and economic conditions and securing their elementary rights as workers, at the time of World War II the Italian fascist regime was heavily engaged in fierce competition with the other European colonial forces to implement its expansionist plan in the region. It was therefore unthinkable for the Eritrean workers to exercise any nationalist political agenda in the face of the brutal racist policy and massive forcible military conscription of the Eritrean youth that the fascist regime was enforcing.

After the fascist reign in Eritrea came to an end in 1941 when Italy was defeated by the Allied Forces, the Eritrean people's aspiration for national freedom became highly charged, especially among the conscious strata composed of workers and the educated. Thus the Eritrean workers' movement was transformed from its narrow enclave of workers' rights to playing an active role in the national and political matters.

However, during the 1941-1949 after the decisive conclusion of World War II the British administration embarked upon a policy of dismembering Eritrea to implement its long awaited plot of enlarging its colonies by adjoining parts of Eritrea. In order to justify its project the British administration descended on the weakening of the Eritrean economy by plundering and destroying vital infrastructure and industries. This resulted in the suffering of the Eritrean works from massive unemployment and disintegration that caused great setback to the organization and movement of the Eritrean workers.

The British Military Administration in Eritrea was replaced in 1949 by a civilian administration that introduced new changes in the existing colonial laws and system of administration. The newly introduced liberal changes gave Eritrean people an opportunity to participate in political and civic activities. It also gave the Eritrean workers an opening to revive their organization and to advocate for their rights taking advantages of the newly instituted labour Code and a labour supervisory office. Thus the period from 1949 until the establishment of a federal system of government in Eritrea in 1952 the Eritrean workers were preoccupied in a series of strikes in order to ascertain their rights.

For instance, the strike waged by the dock workers in Massawa that lasted for six months in March and April 1949 was one of the notable industrial actions of the time. This strike combined political and economic demands that were formally submitted by the worker's representatives to the British administrator in Eritrea. The event was significant in that it forced the British administration to respond with the formation of the Native Advisory Employment Committee. As a result of the historic strike, the Eritrean workers for the first time secured their right of equal pay for equal work with expatriate workers. Indeed this event occupies a prominent chapter in the history of the Eritrean workers' movement as the first of its kind that forced the colonial administration to concede to workers' demands for their rights to freely organize and bargain with their employers.

In September- November 1952 the workers' associations that were hitherto organized in unions at the level of factories and workshops saw a rapid transformation to a higher level of unionization under the leadership of the veteran Weldeab Weldemariam. The Confederation of Free Eritrean Labour Union was established with its own constitution containing 28 articles. The declaration of the Confederation that it had "no political affiliation of religious connection, and that membership was voluntary and open to all Eritrean workers of any age, sex or religion" is a testimony that it was a progressive worker's organization with far-sighted vision. In accordance with the provision of the Confederation's constitution, the 7th of

December was declared as the Eritrean Workers Day, the first Eritrean workers' day was subsequently marked on the 7th of December 1952 where over 20,000 participants attended. This was an ample evidence of the powers and popularity that the Eritrean workers' association commanded at the time.

The Ethio-Eritrean federal administration was put to effect in 1952. Soon, the imperial government of Ethiopia took measures in 1953-1954 to put under the government sector the big economic establishments such as transportation, communication and many others that employed large numbers of workers. This measure that brought their workers under government administration and control was the first move designed to curtail the Eritrean workers' movement and to undermine their rights early on. In January 1954 the Eritrean dock workers in Massawa and Assab staged strikes opposing the moves.

During the period from 1954 to 1958 the nominal government of Eritrea led by Asfaha Woldemichael and the emperor's special envoy in Eritrea, Andergachew Messai exercised their hostilities against the free existence of the Eritrean workers' associations using the Eritrean parliament that was dominated by the unionist elements. In March 1958 which gave powers to the leader of the Eritrean government to reject and dismiss workers associations. The Eritrean workers tried to peacefully oppose the ratification of the employment act, specifically against article 84 which gave the leader of the government such powers. However, since their peaceful efforts did not bear fruition, during 10-30 March 1958 the Eritrean workers staged huge strikes that paralyzed the economic activities of major towns causing nation-wide instability.

Although the infringement of workers' freedom to organize was the apparent cause of the strikes, the actual aim of the massive demonstrations staged by workers, students and other segments of the society was to oppose the economic plunder and political repression perpetrated by Ethiopian and thus to demand national independence. The brutal force with which the Ethiopian regime reacted against the peaceful demonstrations served as a big turning point that transformed the Eritrean workers' movement and the Eritrean people's struggle for independence to a stage that was new both in form and content. Starting from September 1961, therefore, the Eritrean workers' movement became an integral part of the Eritrean people's struggle for national liberation and independence.

It is not possible, in the space of this article, to attempt to explain the organizational development ant the role played by the Eritrean workers in the course of the 30 years bloody armed struggle. For the time being, it is prudent to mention that the Eritrean workers' have been a highly charged and disciplined force whose dedication finds no matching anywhere in the world. Starting from 1961 until they were organized on November 1979 under the umbrella of the National Union of Eritrean Workers (NUEW) the Eritrean workers in Ethiopia and inside Eritrea, as well as those living in exile in all corners of the world continued to pay heavy toll that made significant contributions towards the realization of the Eritrean just cause.

Starting from 1979 until the realization of Eritrea's independence the Eritrean workers residing in all corners of the world organized in the National Union of Eritrean Workers (NUEW) under the umbrella of the Eritrean People's Liberation Front (EPLF) or individually waged relentless struggle for the workers' rights, as well as for the attainment of the Eritrean people's aspirations for independence and the right for self-determination. Ever since Eritrea's independence in 1991 the Eritrean workers have been occupied in the strengthening of their organization in order to safeguard their interests and rights, and to secure the sovereignty of the country and to develop its economy.

Efforts exerted to find peaceful solution

Why did the Eritrean people resort to armed struggle?

The Eritrean people resort to armed struggle mainly because all efforts made to gain its independence through peaceful means were exhausted. And the armed struggle for independence continued until the Eritrean people gained its independence and be able to decide its state of affairs by its own. That, however, does not mean that no efforts have been made to resolve its state of affairs through peaceful means. It has been pushing rigorously for peaceful solution for it knows that a lot could be gained from that.

The EPLF's bidding for peace emanates from this perception. And it made different contacts in several places with the Dergue regime in a bid to resolve the Eritrean issue through peaceful means. The contacts made in East Germany and in other European countries attest to the efforts made. The referendum proposal presented by the EPLF in 1980 also demonstrates how much the front was ready for peaceful solution. Many peace loving nations and organizations have demonstrated their support. It still stand firm in its stance and that has been practically demonstrated in 1993.

To the contrary the Dergue regime was using the peaceful solution for deceiving and intimidation. For the Dergue regime, to resolve the issue of Eritrea through peaceful means, means to lay arms and surrender. Peaceful means for the regime was only to buy time to reinforce itself when things go against it. Hence, all efforts made by the EPLF to find peaceful solution could not bear fruit.

Eritrea Constitutional Governance

Democracy means different things to different cultures and mostly contested term and it is often more in name only than genuine. Democracy as we see it in the developing nations has lead to blunder, ethnic killing and religious war. Eritrea wants none of this nonsense. Eritrea's governance is based on equality, justice, diversity in unity and quality of life. Political reforms include more substantive principle. What we need is Governance with constitutional constraints, tailored to local realities and a government that is devoted to its people and increase opportunity. Eritrea does have leaders, institutions, social forces and effective, efficient and genuine leadership with high administrative skill to bring the nation into prospers civil and modern nation.

In his book The coming Anarchy, Kaplan states; "Democracy or free election should come after free market had produced enough economic and social development to make democracy sustainable. Middle class and civil institutions are precondition for stable democracy and are bi-product of a free market". He goes on to say " Contrasting Lee Kuan Yew's prosperous authoritarian Singapore with the killings, "bloodletting democratic states of Columbia, Rwanda, and South Africa, Kaplan strongly criticizes America's post-Cold War undertaking to export democracy abroad, to places where it can't succeed". Great political thinkers and sociologists have for many years argued that Economic prosperity should press free election; in 1959, noted sociologist Seymour Martin and in 1968 political scientist Samuel P. Huntington both argued strongly against rapid democratization in the developing modernizing societies. Young Third Word economists are in agreement with the idea of economic prosperity first democracy later.

Eritrea is different in the sense that it's a country that came with shared sacrifices, family values and the individual exists in the context of the family rather than the western value of individualism. As a nation it has no minorities' who dominates the economy, equality is the motto. Eritrea after independence started rebuilding its economy; had attained remarkable progress in its economy and was working on a political transition to be governed by constitutional governance. These progresses were interrupted by Ethiopia's war of aggression. Ideals of self reliance became a cause for other nations to gang up on Eritrea to divert the nation from its economic and political development. Eritrea did not blink; it diverted its resources to generate growth. Socioeconomic reforms were put in place "leveling the playing field' social justice educational opportunities were expanded, to the rural areas to bring the impoverished majority to compete successfully with the urban rich. Health services were expanded to reach the most remote area, infrastructures were built: roads, bridges, water diversion skims, dams, and water reservoirs were built to enhance food security. Transportation services were expanded to villages. Education being the engine of economic development has been expanded. Universities and colleges were built and presently expanding. Boarding schools were introduced in the remote and dispersed area of the country. National Cooperation's were formed where the nationals benefit from ownership and capital. Encourage equity to develop through sales of shares and encourage single ownership involve not only efficiency gains but also a more open society. Wealth balances through intervention on behalf of an economically disadvantage group is in place owing to progressive taxation. The sum of all begets a wealthy nation fulfilling the prerequisite for a stable Democratic country.

History has taught us that democracy emerged in the Western nation gradually over centuries and incrementally, over many generations. Yet it's being forced upon developing nations overnight without consideration. Majority rule or democracy is not and must not be the priority; constitutional safeguards, protection and guaranties against arbitrary government confiscation and human rights protection should be the main concern. One man one vote may not be the best system or parliamentarian proportional representation may not fit Eritrea. Bottom-up democratization local village election may be the best way to transfer into democracy. Eritrea's Political reforms are gaining ground. In Eritrea there are open local village elections and district election in cities, there might be some limitations however the election offers a vital measure of political participation and more significantly, legitimate competitive election as an important part of the political process. There have been many improvements in granting the great majority of citizens far more economic and personal freedoms than they have enjoyed since the war of aggression by Ethiopia and its handlers.

The nation has attained urbanization, political modernization and secular nationals. Eritrea has no difficulty in implementing democracy. EPLF ideals were to first free the nation from its colonizers, second to develop the country economically and third to attain a democratic nation. These were and remain to be the mission and visions of the Eritrean people and leaders

Independence Eritrea [The Silver Jubilee]!

In this month of May, Eritrea is celebrating its Silver Jubilee of Independence, which is a sensational tribute to our fallen martyrs. It is a historic record, where Eritreans fought against giant forces for more than half a century, to define their self-determination. The struggle for independence is a testimony to the strong resistance of Eritreans against relentless and all kinds of fabricated aggressions. Eritrea`s heroes/ heroines gave their precious lives for the possibility of this nation, under a strong and vigorous leadership. The sacrifices and commitments of these fighters alongside the fearless people were historically unique and a big lesson to the giant oppressors.

The struggle for independence was unbearable; however, there was a dream that one day this nation would rise up and prosper. A dream which has turned to reality through mass-participation on the 24th of May of 1991, 25 years to this day

Now, 25years later, a distinguished national event of our independence is being celebrated nationwide, in strong vibes and sentiments based on a deep-rooted culture of pride of its citizens. The jubilance magnifies the home-grown traditions of commonality, resilience and sacrifice, grasped during the long course of the struggle for independence. Eritrea and its people are celebrating in a strong zeal, enthusiasm, and pride, in exclusively public centered festivities. The celebrations may look like simple music concerts for many; however, the meaning is beyond imagination.

It is a sign of triumph that maintains the solidarity of its people by orchestrating the unique sense of togetherness of its people towards a nation building process. We Eritreans celebrate our nation as being exceptionally ethical and confidently contend that dignity; fairness and a unique sense of nationalism are what differentiate us from other societies.

The celebration of our independence is valuable as it is bounded by extraordinary reminiscences which are not yet known and /or narrated to the world. The long year's battle for freedom had left an unforgettable impact on the Eritrean society. It is not possible to disclose the miraculous history of the Eritrean struggle for independence in this short paper; meanwhile, it is worth mentioning some bold points. The Eritrean struggle for independence was: (i) involving every family, ethnic and religious group, who represented the entire Eritrean society without discrimination; (ii) a struggle, based on exclusive mass-participation and dynamic leadership, (iii) a struggle that whitewashed the World Community denial to Eritrea`s independence; (iv) a struggle, that culminated the hideous religious discriminations introduced by opportunistic colonizers; (v) a struggle, that women affirmed and secured their equality for the first time in the country`s political history; (vi) a struggle, with 99.83 % vote in favor of independence that assured the well-built solidarity and self-esteem of its nine ethno-linguistic groups.

Within the last 25 years of post-independence, Eritrea`s sovereignty has been unequivocally violated. For a decade and a half, Eritreans condemned the continued military presence from the neighboring country (Ethiopia) in our sovereign land, after signing the final and binding Algiers Peace Treaty on 18 June 2000. However, despite Ethiopia's violation of the rule of law, the International Community (UNSC) and its allies intimidated Eritrea`s sovereignty with fallacious allegations to deviate the right path to development. But, this has not been unanticipated to the Eritrean people, who have been spent more than half a century fighting evil atrocities and fictitious accusation.

The Eritrean people melted together into a harmonious whole with a common cultural struggle and fought vigorously for their identity, peace and sovereignty. They cultivated a home-grown brand of democracy, by the people and for the people. This democracy fostered self-reliance, mutual cooperation and secured sovereignty, peace, and development which is incomparable and provides an exemplary historic record for the region.

However, this kind of democracy was a threat to the aggressors and their allies. They tried to demolish ours and plant their own conjured democracy, in order to throw the Eritrean people again into never-ending hardships and poverty. The corrupt political agenda in our region was unquestionably deceiving our people and sadly it is not organic. This baloney political agenda is manufactured and politically imported by cold-hearted superpowers and manipulative societies, lately obediently implemented by treacherous allies in the region. However, once again the Eritrean People is re-affirming, "If war with Eritrea was difficult yesterday, it is impossible today".

Eritrea's crystal-clear resource is its people, and historically it is proven. The Eritrean people died more than once for the country they loved, and defended their identity with sweat and blood. During those hard times, that is, when even the stones were burning, everything was against us; likewise the same people are now challenging superpowers. At this very moment, these people are celebrating their Silver Jubilee of Independence with pride and dignity. The people are expressing their jubilance, remembering the valuable prices paid in each second of every step they take.

The struggle is still continuing with the same vibe of solidarity, vigilance, and resilience against continuous repulsive fabrications, in order to create a better Eritrea and to sustain the well-being and quality of life of its people.

An Expense for Life of All!

The struggle for freedom was indeed a great deal of sacrificing valiant young patriots who were visionaries and powerful minded, who could have contributed more after liberation of the nation. Life sometimes runs contrary to how things are supposed to be, but the fact that we might not even gain anything regardless its size and quality had we not sacrificed what is valuable in our lives.

To this our veterans devoted too much of their lives to bring our nation a light from the long storm of harsh colonialism. The idea of handing Eritrea to the benefit of the colonizing regimes and the coldblooded Derg military juntas an unorganized agenda of dismantling Eritrea from the base of its existence was meant to have unreturned free access to the Red Sea for the aggressors. Our martyrs saw the need for an independent Eritrea and what it meant to get it, they tasted and felt the freedom of liberation without seeing it, but most of all assumed that if they were caught by the first bullet in the field, their other peers might get greater chance of seeing the glory of liberty.

A sacrifice of your life for your partner to live! It was not a difficult intention to hold, back then. Because every patriot was ready to give up their life for the sake of their partner to continue the battle against unjustified war of expansion and brutal barbaric mental exploitation. "Sacrifice", for Eritreans is a very noble standard with noble ends like freedom and absolute independence of identity and nation. The outcome of all the endeavour comes to be a liberation day and the creation of a sovereign and secured nation Eritrea. What was once a vision of an undefined occurrence had finally become a reality. The bloodshed of our martyrs and their aim to free Eritrea and save the historic identity was not a bargaining ship for both our patriots late and alive. Taking into consideration the battle of "Ghinda", many patriots of the frontline had to sacrifice their lives fighting to liberate the city by walking through the enemy's bomb barricades, to open the gates through the mountains for their units to continue the battle.

Defining what sacrifice had meant for fellow veterans back in the battle field with simple words is not an easy task. For it meant more than just giving up their life to defend the nation's salvation. It had far greater meaning, it was to defend the identity that had been so many times exposed to abduction by foreign colonizing political parties and claim the existence of Eritrea's historical identity. The abduction of its identity was a strategy meant to collide and join Eritreans with other ethnicities and slowly disintegrate them out of their own historic background. Fighting to save the identity and create their own history despite the history of annexation they faced for long was their vision of every martyr, it was a massive vote of 'NO' to suppression and conquest.

Even after liberation freedom fighters carried on the responsibility of rebuilding their home nation and beware against alerts of further disputes. The feeling of readiness to defend the nation remains a permanent foundation in every patriot's mind pre and post-independence. Some freedom fighters I happen to meet explained to me if we went back to the armed struggle to see the rate of readiness to sacrifice was more than salvation, it was simply providing a partner a chance to see tomorrow and just continuing to fight, literally to proceed where the others have left off.

Here is another candle to light for the commemoration of a freedom fighter who is remembered by his partners back in the fields. He passed away long after liberation. He is one of those who played a part in Eritrea's development and reconstruction, contributing in the best way he knows how. This year I chose to pay a tribute to the late freedom fighter Engineer Mehreteab Tesfagerghis who was among the many gallant heroes and heroine martyrs.

Mehreteab Tesfagergis was a veteran, a freedom fighter who had joined the EPLF in 1976 and set his feet until 1991 day of emancipation. He was one of those who created the radio of the Masses "Demsi Hafash" in 1979 in the liberated zone of "Fa'h" Sahel. In fact he was a Technical creator and innovator who developed the transmission capacity of the radio station and its studios until it was able to successfully reach and clearly cover almost all neighbouring countries and beyond, during the armed struggle.

After liberation, the Department of Information came to Asmara from the mountains of "Hager Nish", where it was based during the liberation struggle. Almost after three years an idea of building a new premises for the Ministry of Information was enacted to be on the top hill of "Forto", where it is currently located.

By that time new big radio transmitters were brought and television broadcasting launched. So Engineer Mehreteab saw the need of implanting a higher tower to transmit from the studios over the hill of "Forto" to where the radio receivers in "Sela Daro" and "Biet Gergish" are placed in the direct line of its sight. He searched everywhere for a higher tower until he came to find one placed and used by the "Kagnew station", a residential camp in Asmara after liberation, which was a former camp base for American soldiers in the time of Hailesilasie Administration. It was called 'Track B' tower, the Engineer then dismantled it and reinstalled it on the official base of the Ministry at Forto. Ever since, it has been doing perfect performance in transmission and connecting flows of radio and television broadcasting from the studios at the Ministry of information to the above mentioned towns.

Beyond becoming available worldwide it has a frequency of its own in international cables of Arab Sat and Nile Sat. One of his colleagues told me, "when I look at the tower lit in red and yellow at the top of the hill I always remember my veteran colleague innovator Engineer Mehreteab."

On the other hand that was not the only achievement he had accomplished. Engineer Mehreteab Tesfagerghis put a great impact in developing and enhancing the Eritrean Telecommunication (Eritel). His devotion and the devotion of many others like him have brought many things to light and growth.

People like Engineer Mehreteab sacrificed the blossoming years of their teenage lives for the sake of national prosperity and lived to add to it afterwards with great dedication. When it came to sacrifice for freedom and the grace of a nation, they even continued sacrificing to create a far brighter future for young generations like mine and the next ones. For they will always be the generation that planted pride, determination and resilience in the heart of every Eritrean, as so their history will remain to prosper far into the future.

Foreign Political and Diplomatic Activities

In today's world, political developments, international relations, wars, conflicts, treats, economic relations and cultural exchanges increasingly influence each other and no political phenomenon or movement should be seen in isolation. To properly asses the EPLF's diplomatic activity during the struggle, therefore, it is necessary to analyze the international and regional political atmosphere under which it was undertaken.

Among the factors that influence political developments in the world, the deceive ones are the big powers. These powers in the first instance the

United States and the Soviet Union were powerful and influential on account of their economic and military and hence their political right. Their power, however, does not derive solely from their own resources, but is buttressed by that of their allies and followers.

The world was generally presented as divided in to two camps representing different socio-economic systems. But this assessment doesn't reflect the objective political situation of the world. The two camps were not divided on the basis principal and ideology, but on the basis of the struggle for spheres of influence.

The EPLF realized that the pervasive influence of the two super-powers, their opposition to the Eritrean people'sright to self-determination and their contention in the region were the causes not only of the suffering of Eritrean people but also of conflict and instability in the Horn of Africa. The EPLF, therefore, reputedly called on the Soviet Union to recognize the rights of the peoples of the Horn to decide independently their destinies and to use their influence to advance the causes of peace and instability in the region.

United States of America

The role and influence of the US in the world can be analyzed under three topics: economic, military and political.

Over the last 50 years the economic influence of the U.S has been on the rise. It is the leading country of monopoly capital and its economic dominance in the world on its industrial, technological and trade capacity.

American companies have increasingly dominated nationally or regionally based companies in other continents. Most independent companies in other industrial countries cannot compete with their American rival in size, capacity and capital investment and were therefore dominated by the

American giants. Moreover, many other companies in the developed world are U.S subsidiaries, set up wholly or in part by American capital and technology.

In terms of man power too, the specialist, professionals as well as skilled and other workers of the developed countries directly or indirectly serve American industries, financial institutions and multi-national companies. American scientific, technological and industrial innovations are supplemented by similar break-throughand developments in other industrial countries.

The U.S domination total or partial of the industrial development of Japan, the Far East, Western Europe, Canada and Australia that started in earnest after the Second World War has grown steadily over the past ten years spurred on by meteoric technological advances. There is an aspect of competition in the relation between the U.S and other capitalist countries. But this is secondary and does not constitute a significant factor obstructing U.S domination of the world capitalist system.

Compared with the developed countries, the level of industrial development and economic independence of the semi-developed countries of Asia, Latin America and Africa was very low and highly dominated by the U.S and the other developed nations. The industries of semi-developed countries remain an appendage of those of the U.S.A and U.S dominated developed countries due to the low level of education and technological development of the semi-developed countries and because the advanced industrial nations feel threatened by and therefore block their independent and technological growth.

The underdeveloped countries, of Asia, Africa and Latin America usually referred to as the "Third World" are countries which boast of no significant industrial development. Most are either friends or followers of America and its allies. In the world economy, they play the role of sources of raw materials and cheap labor, and that of consumers. As dependencies and backyards they serve to strengthen the U.S and other developed countries. The growth of American domination on the Third World was manifested in the ever deepening economic crisis that has be set "developing" countries.

The economic dominance of the U.S. and its partners created major problem. American technological progress brought about a high rate of unemployment in the developed countries and more poverty and crisis in the semi-developed and under-developed countries. More unemployment, poverty and economic crisis on a world-level bound to follow.

The American domination of world trade was a projection of its industrial dominance. Although attempts were made to regulate trade between the U.S. on the one hand, and Japan, Australia, the developed countries of the Far East, Western Europe and Canada on the other through tariff and trade agreement, financial and commercial might eventually tilt the balance in America's favor.

Therefore, American dominance and control of world trade was growing steadily.

The trade relationship between the semi-developed and the underdeveloped countries and the U.S.A and other developed nations was not based on equality and mutual benefit. Most of the former were debt-ridden. Wehave seen many countries burdened by huge debts and interest payments which they cannot meet. Moreover the general trend in international trade which boosted the growth and dominance of the American economy created friction between U.S.A and its allies

For the US, military superiority was essential for the protection of its strategic economic interests. It therefore, devoted huge resources industrial, financial and human to the production of weapons. The time has seen not only an increase in U.S nuclear capability but the developments of a weapon system in space (Star Wares), which was based on the use of the result of scientific and technological research in space for military purpose. These developments raised American military superiority and negotiating power.

American efforts to militarily strengthen client states have been growing. The consideration of the NATO alliance, the deployment of new nuclear weapons in Western Europe, the upgrading of the NATO members' capacity to produce nuclear weapons, and the consolidation of NATO air, naval and ground conventional forces were indicators of American military thinking. The U.S. also attempting to strengthen regional alliances and individual client states through increased military aid to enable them, in the absence of direct American interference, to defend themselves and act as regional watchdogs. And in case this strategy fails, the U.S had its military bases and Rapid Deployment Forces which it has been strengthening for years. Moreover as the invasion of Grendada and the Libyan air raids show U.S disinclination to resort to direct military interference.

An aspect of U.S military strategy that has become more pronounced over the years was indirect military intervention, the support of opposition groups, where this do not exist, the creation, organization and financing of groups to fight Anti-American states. It supported to the contras in Nicaragua, UNITA in Angola and the Mujahedeen in Afghanistan in a manifestation of this policy, a policy which was supplemented by CIA espionage, sabotage, terrorism and assassination.

The American government claims to stand for liberty, brotherhood, equality, democracy and human rights in order to protect its worldwide interests. The policy of racial discrimination against Blacks and Native Americans, the violation of the social, economic and political rights of large sections of the population in Western Europe, the emergence of extreme right-wing and neo-fascist groups and the elimination of moderate and democratic forces by terror and sabotage were phenomena that give the lie to American claims.

The U.S. world political strategy can also be perceived from the type of regimes that are found in the semi-developed and under- developed Asian, African, and Latin American countries. Most of those allied with the U.S.A were military, monarchist and fascist dictatorships abhorred by their peoples. Moreover, those countries that establish true and democratic systems were subjected to US engineered coups, military pressure and economic sanctions.

In the decades, the US has adopted a new foreign policy tactic.

When extremely notorious regimes are threatened by popular uprising, the Americans promptly before things go out of hand replace the unpopular leaders, leaving the regime intact. Moreover, the Americans goad client governments to carry out reforms to blunt popular opposition and ensure their survival.

It is the responsibility of international and regional organizations like the U.N. and the O.A.U. to prevent human rights violations and invasions and solve conflicts. But among other causes, American domination virtually paralyzed these bodies. The U.S. uses its international influence to prevent the cases of the oppressed from being raised in those bodies and to ensure their rejection if they are raised. It also pressures these international forums into passing resolutions that favor it. And when it does not suit its interest, the US by passes these bodies and resorts to force to solve the problem it faces. As a result bloody conflicts and injustices that have continued for a decade and more have not found proper solutions. The Eritrean case was one of many examples.

Valuation of EPLF's familiarity in the period between its 1st and 2nd Congress

The EPLF's mission is the realization of the Eritrean people's right to self determination and independence. This was reaffirmed in clear terms in its national democratic program adopted at its first congress. But the struggle to emancipate the Eritrean people from the colonial yoke of oppression requires not only waging a war of liberation against the colonial army but entails a comprehensive political struggle and all-round nation building tasks. Shouldering this responsibility and recognizing its importance, the EPLF accomplished many tasks in various fields, gaining in the process a rich experience and bringing about tangible changes. In the following the changes will be discussed in accordance with their importance. Political work among the masses

Ever since Eritrea emerged as a nation especially over the past 40 years, the task of raising the national consciousness of the Eritrean people so it would be on par with the process of nation building has remained fundamental. This task includes the fostering of a common national consciousness by eliminating sectarian sentiments emanating from the backward social and economic structure of the Eritrean society; the development of a nationwide political organization by discarding the narrow and backward organizational forms thrown up by the backward social formation; and the guaranteeing of the broad and democratic participation of the masses in the liberation struggle and national reconstruction.

In order to realize these political objectives stage by stage, the EPLF strove to raise the political consciousness of the Eritrean people so that a common nationalism would subsume religious, provincial, tribal and ethnic sentiments. It also worked to enable the people to organize themselves in national associations based on social standing, set up popular institutions on democratic bases to replace those serving traditional leaders and arm themselves to protect their democratic gains.

To raise the political consciousness of the people, regular political education was introduced. Topics such as history of the Eritrean people and their struggle, the correct national line and methods of struggle, basic political concepts, forms of colonialism, its collaborators and their tactics, developments of the international political scene, rights and obligations of the masses, democratic organizational principles, perseverance, etc., were discussed. These discussions were not limited to

EPLF members, but public meetings and seminars were organized so the population at large could participate and help in broadening and deepening understanding of the issues. Towards the same end, books were translated, journals and other publications widely disseminated. A radio station-The Voice of the Masses-was also set up to assist in the politicization of the masses, particularly those who live in inaccessible areas. Research was carried out in the economic, social and cultural life and the folklore of the Eritrean people so political work would be based on Eritrean reality.

The second aspect of EPLF's political work pertains to mass organizations. Here its fundamental policy to organize the Eritrean masses on the basis of their social status into associations of workers, peasants, women, students as well as professionals. The political work was effective and the associations held their founding congress, declared their programs, elected their leadership and have been actively broadening and consolidating their ranks. Parallel with this and on the basis of the Front's policy of setting up democratic political and administrative bodies inside the country, people's assemblies were formed at village and district levels in the liberated and semi-liberated areas and were functioning properly. To simplify their administrative work, committees responsible for cooperatives, economic life, justice, etc, were elected and as a result the people's role in self-administration improved.

The third policy objective was arming the people. In many regions, village and district people's militia were formed. These have not only been defending their institutions and revolutionary gains, but they have also confronted the enemy's military offensives and campaigns in conjunction with regional and regular units of the People's Army.

The tasks of politicizing, organizing and arming the population was not carried out without obstacles and shortcomings. Naturally, the major obstacle was the colonial Dergue regime and its political designs. Although there was no strata of Eritrean society collaborating with colonial regime, the Dergue had not stopped its attempts at deception. Failing in this, it had resorted to preventing our people from listening to "Voice of the Masses" broadcasts and reading EPLF publications, further revealing it political bankruptcy. The obstruction caused by the colonialist regime is due to its fascist repressive measures more than its political campaigns. It had deprived the Eritrean people of the basic rights of assembly and speech, employed the Kebele institutions which serve as a security and police apparatus to restrict their freedom of movement and obstruct their efforts at organization, and imprisoned and executed active EPLF members. To prevent the youth from joining the national struggle it exposes them to corruptive influences and conscript them into its colonial army. In the rural areas, it carries out military incursions, acts of sabotage and aerial bombardment to destroy popular institutions, disrupt the peace and displace the population. During the years of drought, the Dergue took deliberate measures to ruin the already fragile economy and utilized food aid as a means of political control. Lastly, in an attempt at legitimacy, it forced our people to vote at gun point in a constitutional referendum which had no relevance to their case. Although these measures did not dampen the Eritrean people's aspiration for independence, they obstructed the EPLF's task of establishing and strengthening popular democratic institutions. Nevertheless our people have been able to preserve, adopt new forms of organization, set-up clandestine institutions and even work from within the Dergue's police-like institutions, such as the Kebeles.

The second obstacle was that created by the internal forces of reaction. As the Eritrean people's struggle matured and the old ideas and sectarianism flagged the elements that had an interest in fanning ethnic, religious and regional differences and who felt threatened by EPLF's policy of politicizing, organizing and arming the people dished out what they felt were the most appealing arguments and employed all the means at their disposal to sow distrust and mutual resentment so as to maintain the factional groupings the could freely manipulate. The weaker they go the more they desperate they became in their efforts-especially abroad-to confuse the masses and prevent them from actively supporting the EPLF. These groups which cannot survive on their own, were trying vainly to prolong their existence with the support of foreign powers and by exploiting the economic and social problems of Eritrean refugees. The problem of internal reaction was a long term problem that disappeared in the process of nation-building and the growth of the active political participation of the masses. Seen in this light and taking into consideration the developments of the past which saw active mass participation and a rapid growth of the people's confidence in the EPLF, the harm caused by the irresponsible campaigns of the internal reactionaries, was while undeniable, extremely limited.

The massive displacement of the Eritrean people was another factor that affected our political and organizational activities. In the 1977-78 period, when large areas of Eritrea were liberated and an open and democratic atmosphere prevailed popular institutions flourished in the rural areas as well as in the towns. This aroused the hope of Eritrean refugees to return home and participate in national reconstruction and popular participation received a tremendous boost. With the strategic withdrawal the active elements were forced to flee and emigrate. This adversely affected life and living condition in the areas retaken by the enemy, particularly the town. Unemployment and the lack of secure life became unbearable. Drought and instability wrought havoc on agricultural and livestock production and became additional burden on an already untenable situation.

Because it takes an extended period to change the military balance of forces, and since inside Eritrea, the question of survival became the primary concern while abroad ensuring sanctuary and social security, securing the means to support oneself and dependents was a necessity, the high level of participation in the struggle flagged through national aspirations and sentiments remained intact. Popular participation was also negatively affected by the Dergue's suppression and destruction and the reactionary forces' defeatist propaganda.

In the setting up and consolidation of mass organizations and popular institutions, the training of competent cadres and the devising of effective working methods are basic. The task, however, was not the responsibility only of the Department of Mass Administration, but also falls on other EPLF institutions. Although the Department of Mass Administration had taken the training of cadres and the continuous improvement of organizational forms and working methods as its main tasks, there were shortcomings in the capacity of its cadres. Another drawback was the failure of other EPLF departments and sections to always coordinate their specific tasks with the ongoing activities among the people.

Though not isolated from EPLF's overall political work among the masses, the efforts to promote the role of women were of special interest. Since the participation of all nationals in the process of liberating and developing Eritrea was an imperative task, the participation of women, who make up half of our society, must be given great attention. It is easy to accept this in principle and grasp its theoretical importance, but it is difficult to turn it into a reality. It is hard to persuade a backward male dominated society, fettered by chauvinist and superstitious beliefs that consider women as weak and ignorant, and relegates them to second class citizenship to accept that women are equal to men. But the EPLF incorporated women's rights and their participation in its political programs and worked seriously to implement it. The advances made by women in their politicization, training, the setting up of their own association, their substantial role in the armed struggle and the exemplary heroism they demonstrated, their important representation in the people's assemblies, their participation in agriculture and other productive activities, their active role in the fields of education and health, the upgrading of their administrative and leadership capabilities, in short their participation in all aspects of the Eritrean revolution are tangible and practical proofs of the correctness of the EPLF policy and the seriousness with which it was implemented. Even though, many shortcomings which can be traced to the backwardness of our society, shortage of time and limited experiences have been to be corrected, the participation of women, which the Eritrean people are proud of, had solved many problems and had simplified future tasks.

Expansionism in the Horn

Following the Berlin conference of 1884-1885, European powers divided up Africa among themselves and throughout the continent, the process of nation formation began within the colonial boundaries. In the Horn of Africa, France occupied French Somaliland now known as Djibouti; Britain took over British Somaliland, now part of the Republic of Somalia, and Italy took possession of Eritrea as well as Italian Somaliland which is now part of the Republic of Somalia; Ethiopia, however, did not fall under the colonial yoke, partly because of the resistance of the north and partly due to the agreement of competing colonial powers on future goals.

Italian colonialism in Eritrea

The Italian colonialists had special aims in Eritrea. Their objectives were not confined to exploiting Eritrea's natural and human resources but extended to occupying a large territory in the Horn of Africa- including Ethiopia. Towards this end, they gave primacy to turning Somalia and especially strategically-located Eritrea into spring boards for their invasion of Ethiopia. They invested large amounts of capital in Eritrea and speeded up the dismantling of the traditional economic, social and cultural structures as well as the process of nation-building.

The Italians built ports, roads, railways, and rope ways. They opened airports and introduced sea, land and air transportation. They installed telephone and telegraph networks, established power stations, consumer goods factories and large scale industries. They set up repair and maintenance facilities. They began prospecting for minerals, opened up mines and expanded salt-mining and fishing. They set up large plantations as well as service industries. In short, they introduced a new, advanced, but exploitative, economic system and created new social forces.

The Italians inducted thousands of Eritrean peasants and herdsmen into their colonial army. To meet their administrative needs, they launched a limited educational program confined to teaching the Italian language, the four arithmetic operations and hygiene and began spreading their cultural influence. They made the traditional clan and tribal administration comply with colonial laws. Furthermore, they divided Eritrea into districts and sub-districts, appointed loyal Eritreans to administer them and brought these under the colonial office. They also specified the areas Eritreans could inhabit and freely move in and enacted racially discriminatory laws.

In this manner, Italian colonialism unified Eritrea geographically and set in motion economic; social and cultural changes which in turn fostered common national feeling among Eritreans. Although Italian colonialism proscribed political and trade union rights, this did not prevent-the Eritrean people from mounting strong opposition to Italian policies of exploitation, oppression, racial discrimination and forcible conscription. Many Eritreans fled to Ethiopia. It was then that Nacura became a notorious prison.

Political and military struggle, Anti Colonialism

First Part

The national struggle of the Eritrean people was a fight against "Ethiopian" colonial regimes which were driven by empire building ambitions and supported by international colonialist forces. The struggle continued as long as the imperial dreams and the interests that underlie them persist. The Dergue's regime, its policies and actions should be examined from this perspective. And so has the Dergue's seizure of power brought change in Ethiopia?

A regime could be substituted by another and there could be difference in form and style between one regime and another. However, change in the system could only occur if there is a transformation of its essence. A snake does not cease to be a snake because, it has molted.

The backward and autocratic regime of Haile Selassie with the support of world colonialist forces, trampled on the fundamental human and democratic rights and particularly the national rights of the people of Ethiopia so as to ensure the dominance of one nationality, the Amhara. In addition, it strove to colonialize the people of Horn of Africa and especially Eritrea in order to realize its expansionist dreams. It also appropriated the wealth and in the first place the land of the Ethiopian people turning into the private property of the imperial family and the feudal aristocracy and causing misery. It was therefore, natural that the struggles of the Eritrean people and the peoples of Ethiopia should over throw the regime of Haile Selassie. But did the fall of Haile Selassie achieve the objectives of the struggles? This is a question that can only be answered by examining the Dergue, its policies.

Briefly speaking, if there was anything the Dergue had attempted to strengthen the efforts at empire-building which it inherited from Haile Selassie. At first the Dergue found it expedient to condemning the misery of the Ethiopian people. Not because it upheld the legitimate causes of the two people but because it was not in a position to confront them head on as it had not yet consolidate its power. Its initial move to institute a hybrid constitutional monarchy by raising the meaning less slogan of "Ethiopia Tikdem" (Ethiopia first) was thwarted by a broad popular opposition. Toward the end of 1974 it raised another equally senseless slogan, that of "Ethiopian Socialism", feeling that this would echo the demands of the people. As the politicalized student body was challenging the regime and agitating against its empty and deceptive slogans, the Dergue introduced in the guise of development and concurrently with its proclamation of "Ethiopian Socialism", the "Zemetcha" (campaign) program and dispersed throughout the country all university and high school students and their teachers. This however, failed to achieve the Dergue's objectives. On the contrary, it facilitated the spreading of the opposition and strengthened the channelings of the regime. In the March 1975, the Dergue issued a proclamation to nationalize rural lands. In the second half of 1975 of July to be exact it proclaimed the expropriation of all urban lands and buildings. It simultaneously initiated the establishment of urban and rural "Kebeles" to better control the popular opposition. As a finale it issued its documentation of "National Democratic Revolution" in the second quarter April of 1976. Towards the end of 1976 (October), the regime convertd the Kebeles into organs of "Red Terror". By then, what the Dergue touted as a "Bloodless Revolution" had turned to be bloody and terroristic.

Second Part

What about the regime's handling of the just and legitimate cause of the Eritrean people? The colonialist Dergue, just like the Haile Selassie regime, did not fail to recognize that the main threat to its expansionist and imperial ambition came from Eritrea. It also realized from the start that it would not crush the Eritrean people's struggle with the weakened state apparatus of Haile Selassie. As the Eritrean case was a burning issue, whose peaceful solution was demanded by the Eritrean people and the people of Ethiopia, the Dergue, as in all other question, hypocritically declared its "readiness" to solve the problem.

As the regime classified 1975 document reveals, however, the corner stone of its policy was to engage in peace maneuvers until such time as it consolidate its power. As it realized that if the Eritrean case with its solid legal grounds was raised on the international agenda "Ethiopia" was bound to loose, the main objective of its foreign policy was one of isolating the Eritrean people's case in the international as well as regional levels. In the event, it set up peace delegations and committees and met with the EPLF and ELF in an attempt at misleading the Eritrean people and the world. And although this initiative raised the hopes of the Eritrean People, who have always struggled for peace, and their organizations, it did not in any way deceive them. Parallel with its feigned peace pronouncements, the Dergue was conducting an extensive and brutal campaign of terror in the cities and rural areas, involving summary executions of innocent civilians by shooting and strangulation and the burning of villages. Even under this circumstance, the Eritrean revolution demonstrated its readiness to inter into dialogue for peace. Furthermore the EPLF sought to find out the Dergue's views on peace so it could also present its proposals and create the conditions for face to face talks. The Dergue, however, was not prepared. When the challenge become so strong as to deny it room for maneuver, the regime resorted to the one solution it envisages for Eritrea and launched its "Red March" offensive. After the failure of this campaign, it proclaimed its Nine Point Policy which was rejected. The Dergue's aim was to engage in hypocritical peace initiatives for public consumption while simultaneously carrying out military preparations to crush the Eritrean revolution.

Consequently the Dergue raised the alarm on a bogus "foreign threat" to induce the Ethiopian people to take up arms to fight in a war they didn't even understood. A second objective of the campaign was to divert the Ethiopian people's attention from its internal opposition. The sharpening of the Ethio-Somali conflict at that time facilitated the deception. The remaining question, that of the acquisition of arms, as solved through Soviet intervention and largesse. The Dergue was, therefore, highly confident, that it would crash the Eritrean revolution. To prepare the grounds that would serve as a pretext for the military offensive, brief, farcical peace talks were conducted in Berlin through Soviet initiative and East German orchestration. When the talks demonstrated that the EPLF would not succumb to pressure and intimidation or betray its cause, the Dergue initiated its large scale offensive. After almost ten years of heavy destruction and blood shade, it became clear that the regime's goals and plans have failed. The experience accumulated in this respect was one among many other things which expose the nature of the Dergue.

The Dergue has trampled on the Ethiopian people's fundamental rights those of speech, movement and organization- and denied them the opportunity to exercise popular power by prohibiting the formation of democratic institutions, and worked to strengthen a "Workers Party" based on the army and the dictatorial police authority or the Kebeles. As a result opposition to the regime and desertion from it had been growing. Since the Dergue does not even trust its main repressive machinery- the military institution and was afraid the army might conduct mutiny or carry out a coup, it emasculated the army's role by miring it in continuous positional warfare in Eritrea and brutally crushing any signs of opposition. The much rehearsed scenario which the Dergue had been enacting as a prelude to proclaiming a "Republic" did not hold anything new. It did not lead to the exercise of the right of nationalities and the establishment of broad popular democracy in Ethiopia, or a political solution to the Eritrean issue. All these clearly show that there was nothing in the nature of the regime to differentiate it from that of Haile Selassie.

Third Part

In his attempt to expand his empire, Haile Selassie depended on foreign assistance. The Dergue too realized that it could not wipe out the Eritrean people's struggle and crush the Ethiopian people's opposition and thus sustain the Ethiopian empire without the support of external forces. From the outset, the Dergue did all it could do to secure American assistance, so it could strengthen the army and meet the threat created by the increased strength of the Eritrean revolution and the Ethiopian peoples' opposition. The U.S. was hesitant in offering arms, not because it was suspicious of the Dergue but because it panicked at the fall of Haile Selassie and at the strength and direction of the opposition which over threw the regime. It did not want to take a hasty step. Badly in need of arms, the Dergue lost patience and did a volt-face turning its attention towards the Soviets. The Soviet Union, which had been watching the developments from afar, quickly took advantage of the new opportunities opened from its global interest, and was only too pleased to deliver arms. In a short period, the Dergue armed forces quadrupled both in numbers and weapons. The intervention of the Soviets and their accomplices wetted the regimes craving for imperial expansions and liquidation of the opposition. This external factor resulted in destruction and bloodshed unprecedented in Eritrean history, prolonged the conflict and blocked other possibilities for resolving the problem.

In addition to stimulating the regime's imperial ambitions on Eritrea, and consolidating dictatorial rule in Ethiopia, the intervention of the Soviet Union and its allies played a major role in destabilizing the region. Leaving aside the military measures taken by Somalia and used as a pretext by Ethiopia, Soviet intervention aroused the Dergues fantasy of becoming a regional power in the ' Horn of Africa and beyond. The Dergue invaded the territory of the Republic of Somalia, in a bid to exploit the problems of Southern Sudan and taking steps against the states in the region to force them to either submit to its domination or face destabilization. These developments not only reflected on the regime's outlook but also revealed the role that the Soviet Union was playing in complicating the politics of the region.

Under these circumstances, which precluded a political solution, what should EPLF have done? And what steps did it take?

In the two terror filled years preceding the first EPLF organizational congress, the nature of the Dergue and the line and direction it had adopted were clearly evident. Its peace maneuvers, the barbaric strangulation of youth and other atrocities it perpetrated on the civilian population in the cities, its burning of villages and massacres in the rural areas such as Weki-Duba and Om-Hajer, the Nine Point Policy, the "Red March" invasion (July 1976), and the large-scale military preparation did not leave room for doubt.

In the first organizational congress, the EPLF assessed the nature of the Deruge regime, decided to vigorously pursue its all-sided struggle, formulated and set out to implement a military strategy of popular liberation and went on the offensive. The town of Karora was liberated on the eve of the first congress (07-01-77). Nakfa (23-03-77) Afabet (06-04-77), Dekmhare (06-07-77), Keren (08-07-77), Segeneiti (03-08-77), Digsa (05-08-77) were liberated in rapid succession. After the Massawa-Asmara high way came under the control of the Eritrean People's Liberation Army on October 12, 1977, Dogali (18-12-1977), parts of Masswa (21-12-77), Dongolo and Ghidae (24-1-78, Embatkala and Maihabar (25-1-78) and Nefacit and Seidici (27-01-78), Agordat (31-08-77), Mendefera (24-8-77), Adi Quala (12-8-77). All rural areas and all Eritrean towns with the exception of Asmara were under siege, partially freed. Massawa as well as Adi Keih, Barentu and Assab, were liberated.

Fourth Part

These developments were a threat not only to the Dergue but also to the allies; the Soviet Union, Cuba, South Yemen, and Libya which intensified their intervention. Soviet delivery of weapons was increased and Cuban and South Yemeni armed forces deployed. The Libyans provided logistical and material support and in the middle of July 1978 a large-scale offensive was launched.

Until then the Eritrean revolution was in the stage of the strategic offensive. The fighting capability of the People's Army and the Peoples Militia was at a high level. But the intervention of the Soviet Union and its collaborators had changed the military balance in the Dergue's favor. Given these developments, it was obvious that the EPLF could not defend all the land it had liberated and safeguarded all of its other gains.

And faced with historical question that demanded correct answer, the EPLF decided to effect a strategic withdrawal, after assessing the military changes which had taken place. But the strategic withdrawal did not imply the losing of hope. At the time comments to the effect that the Eritrean revolution was no more, were common in the international stage. Inside the country, there were those who claimed that it was impossible to confront the enemy's offensive and who accused the EPLF of adventurism. But when EPLF decided on the strategic withdrawal, it did not intend to leave all of the liberated areas at once or go to fragment its forces and return to guerilla warfare. Since the liberation struggle is not only a military task but also political, psychological, social, economic and cultural; and since in liberation war the existence of a base area is of fundamental importance not only for a military objectives but also for conducting the all sided revolutionary's tasks and activities and since establishing a base area outside the boarders in a neighboring country creates dependency and imposes limitation which have negative impact on the revolution, the EPLF decided to ensure the continued existence of a base area, irrespective of size. According to the EPLF strategy, the retreat did not mean taking a leap back to the base area. In the process of the strategic withdrawal, preserving human resources by avoiding unnecessary sacrifices, conserving weapons, inflicting man-power, material and morale loses on the enemy, and, what is more, increasing your fire-power, maintaining and boosting your morale, protecting institutions from destruction so they could later be used for reconstruction and the inevitable counter-offensive the basic elements. Of course, the implementation of such a strategy was not easy. It was a task that demanded heavy sacrifice, fortitude and perseverance. And thanks, to heroism and steadfastness of the people and the EPLF, the objectives of the strategic withdrawal were achieved. In the course of the withdrawal, the People's Army upgraded its battle effectiveness, steeled its morale, increased its fire-power, safeguarded its basic institutions roughly delineated its base area, and went on to ensure a secure defense.

The first phase i.e., the strategic withdrawal- incorporated the first offensive which started in mid-July 1978 with the withdrawal from the South and includes the breaching of the Asmara-Embaderho front up to the battle of Makereka at the end of July; the Second Offensive which began on the 20 November, 1978 and continued till the end of the month in the areas to the east and to the south of Keren; the Third Offensive, starting from January 1979 on the Anseba, Maamide and North Eastern Sahel Fronts and from February 6-9, around Denden on the Nakfa Front; as well as the enemy's futile attempts to breach the various fronts from 30 March up to 11 April 1979 in its fourth Offensive. In the process of withdrawal, the Eritrean Peoples Liberation Army (EPLA) did not only effect a gradual and orderly retreat to its fortifications in Sahel but also intensified its mobile and guerilla operations behind the enemy lines and won important battles. As the enemy had incurred a combined loss of about 25,000 men in the four offensives and the EPLA's defense capability had grown in all respects, the Dergue was forced to make better preparations for its next attempt at breaching EPLA defense lines and liquidating the EPLA in a war of encirclement.

Fifth Part

n the second phase, the EPLA aimed at consolidation while the colonial army's goals were to breach and encircle. After careful preparation and reinforcement of troops, the enemy advanced towards Agrae on 08-07-79 and also mounted simultaneous and continuous attacks on all fronts up to the end of July. However, the offensive was repulsed and the Dergue lost about 12,000 thousand soldiers and an enormous amount of material. In this Fifth Offensive, the enemy also suffered further deterioration in morale. In contrast, the EPLA's confidence and capability to defend its strong hold was enhanced and its fire power boosted.

The strengthening of fortifications and foiling of successive offensives, however, was not sufficient to bring about the necessary levels of consolidation. For this a defensive attack was required and at the beginning of December 1979, the EPLA launched a major counter-offensive on the Nakfa Front driving the enemy forces to the outskirts of Afabet. It also mounted a supportive attack on the North Eastern Sahel Front which dislodged the enemy from its positions and restricted it to the plains. The failure of its five offensives, and the successful counter attacks launched by the EPLA to ensure the defense of the base paralyzed the Dergue's offensive capability as evidence by the two years of parity that followed. Aside from their impact on the military capability of the Dergue, these developments had important political repercussions on the national, regional and international levels. Consequently the

Dergue carried out massive mobilization of men and material for a military adventure. The offensive was preceded by a political campaign in Ethiopia, a political and propaganda offensive in Eritrea aimed at demoralizing the people and an international diplomatic campaign. After successive meetings the Dergue issued the "Asmara Manifesto" to give its offensive a semblance of legality and popular backing.

After all these preparations, the Dergue launched the "Red Star" campaign which it as "the one and final" campaign. The plan of the offensive was to wipe out the EPLF in a two to three week war of encirclement. As prelude to the main attack which commenced on 15-2-1982, the colonial army launched an extensive combined campaign in December 1981 to weaken the EPLA mobile and guerilla units active behind enemy lines. The campaign was frustrated by our forces. The enemy then conducted an intensive aerial bombardment for a whole month. The enemy strategy for the Sixth Offensive was to launch coordinated blitzes on the North East Sahel, Nakfa and Kerkebet (Barka) Fronts. After 18 days of the three prolonged attacks, its armies were expected to rendezvous at Adobha. However, the Dergue's units deployed on the newly opened Barka Front were crushed with heavily losses and the fronts collapsed in the first few days of the offensive. On the remaining two fronts heavy and bitter fighting which tested the mettle of the two armies continued for 95 days and was finally concluded with defeat of the Dergue's army at the end of July. In this offensive the Dergue's casualty amounted to over 40,000. It also incurred immense losses in weapons and other war material. To the EPLF, the 6th offensive was valuable military experience which it surmounted a difficult and trying stage-an important stage which steeled the resolve of the Eritrean people and strengthen the EPLA fighting capability and weapons. It was also a significant political turning point on the international stage.

Sixth Part

The heavy political losses it suffered in the 6th offensive pushed the Dergue to the other suicidal and desperate measures. Mistaking its fantasies for objective reality, the Dergue concluded that the EPLF's manpower had been weakened and its defense capability debilitated by the 6th offensive. It was therefore necessary, the Dergue thought, to attack the EPLF before it got a breathing space and the chance to reinforce. Fooled by the assessments, the Dergue adopted a strategy of attrition to weaken the EPLA in an extended engagement and achieve the objective of the failed 6th offensive.

In marked contrast to the "Red Star Campaign", the Dergue launched the Seventh Offensive (The "Stealth" offensive") at the end of March 1983. This offensive differed from the previous "Red Star" campaign not only its lack of an accompanying fanfare, but its tactics of feinting and stealth, of mounting a concentrated attack in one place and then changing the thrust to another, had nothing in common with the "6th offensive" strategy of attacking on all fronts simultaneously and for a short period. It continued for a record five month until the EPLA seized the initiative and carried out a counter offensive from 6 July up to the middle of August 1983. The Dergue's army suffered a total loss of 25,000 troops in the offensive.

The next stage was characterized by the EPLA's extensive counter offensive. At the beginning of 1984, on the 15th and 16th of January, the Dergue forces in Tessenai and Alighider were attacked and the two towns came under EPLA control. Although a subsequent attack mounted by the EPLA on 22-2-84 against the regime's forces that had entrenched themselves for five years on the North East Sahel Front "Wukaw Command" to the enemy did not succeed, the enemy front was liquidated and an extensive area liberated in a second onslaught from 19-21 March 1984. A successful Commando operation was also carried out on Asmara airport on May 21, 1984.

This extensive counter offensive was continuation and intensification of the mobile and guerilla operations conducted behind enemy lines. As the successful execution of major operations particularly in Western Eritrea led to the contracting of both the areas under the enemy and its defense perimeter, the EPLF decided to mount an attack on Barentu. The operation started on July and the regimes forces were decimated. Operation Barentu inflicted heavy military loses in the colonial army and had major political repercussion which made the Dergue hysterical. To regain the towns, the Dergue mounted continuous counter attacks, and when these proven ineffective, it deployed many additional brigades and brought its biggest mechanized division from the Ogadeh. It subsequently recaptured Barentu on 24, August, 1985 and advanced towards Tessenei retaking the town on 26 August. Although operation Barentu inflicted heavy manpower and material losses on the enemy, boosted the EPLA's firepower and was successful in pre-empting an imminent enemy offensive it did not lead to the strategic consolidation of the EPLA's position.

After barentu, the Dergue reinforced its army in Eritrea by bringing 20,000 conscript of the second round of "National Military Service". Assuming as usual, that the EPLA had been drastically weakened in the battle of Barentu and the regime's "Red Sea" counter-offensive to retake the town and hoping that its return to Barentu and Tessenei has raised the morale of its army the Dergue started a new large-scale offensive calling it "Bahre Negash" on 10-10-85. This offensive, once again touted as "a once and for all" campaign was as usual expect to liquidate the EPLA in a week. In the event, the offensive got bogged down in its first phase, but the Dergue which had already had confidence, launched two more phases, until the EPLA counter attack on 4-12-85 brought the adventure to halt. In this offensive, which turned out to be complete fiasco, the enemy lost a total of 7,000 men.

Seventh Part

In 1986 although the enemy did not undertake any large-scale offensives, it established many outposts and launched small scale campaigns to protect its rear as the EPLF strategy of extensive counter offensive initiated in 1984 and intensified in 1985 had created a serious threat to it. On its part the EPLF had been vigorously pushing and expanding it guerilla and commando operations by penetrating and operating in the cities and extensive rural areas, as well as areas immediately behind the enemy's front lines.

What emerged from the military developments briefly discussed here is that the Dergue's objectives of consolidating its power, of creating and expanding an empire by liquidating by force of arms and a huge army the Eritrean revolution and the movements of the people of Ethiopia have failed. Initially, the Dergue registered military victories because it was able to exploit the prevailing chaos and channel the chauvinistic sentiments it aroused against the Somali attacks, and as a result of the acquisition of Soviet weapons and military advisors and the physical intervention of the Cuban and South Yemeni armies. But there after the Dergue's power and fortunes have been waning. Moreover, as the political bankruptcy of the regime became more evident, the political consciousness and the organized opposition of the Ethiopian people were growing. The failure of the program of national conscription to achieve its numerical targets and successively decreasing number of conscripts from the first to the latest fourth round was a manifestation of the deterioration in the regimes position.

The Dergue's superiority in new weapons played a potent role initially. But not for long. The EPLA narrowed the gap by capturing and achieving proficiency in their use. The Soviet Union, as well as Cuba and South Yemen, who in the beginning has fielded troops, discovered the impracticality of their plan to finish off the war in a matter of months and then congratulate themselves for having "liquidated a counterrevolution". They, there fore, withdrew or reduced their forces in Eritrea and kept low profile. The absence or reduction of their forces which had supplemented the military capability of the colonial army and filled the gaps in its resources and competence further weakened the regime. The continuous deterioration in the army's morale and the existence of a persistent sometimes open at other times latent opposition within the army was another deliberating factor. The spectacle provided by ex-official of the regime who used to plan and applaud its actions and who pronounced in their speeches that "The Eritrean revolution can not be defeated military" was an indication of the general state of affairs.

Eighth Part

The EPLF had, in the course of the heroic struggle for independence, proven many fundamental points. It showed its loyalty to the just struggle of the Eritrean people. It had proven that a just struggle cannot be vanquished no matter how huge the colonial military force (and that of extra force) arrayed against it. It has demonstrated beyond any doubt the correctness of the military strategy it pursued. And the protracted war which has demanded heavy sacrifices, the EPLF has built a people's army with regular, regional and militia units evincing numerical growth., employing sophisticated strategies and tactics, possessing consciousness and morale, well organized, equipped and proficient in light and heavy weapons; dedicated, productive' and a guarantee for the liberation of Eritrea and its reconstruction. The EPLF, however, is not a militarist organization, but a democratic organization which wages an all sided national liberation struggle. It has worked tirelessly for a just and peaceful political solution because it believed this to be the simplest solution, one which minimizes destruction and blood shade and assures peace, prosperity and stability to the people of Eritrea, Ethiopia and the region as a whole.

The Eritrean people's struggle for a just and peaceful political solution went for over 30 years. The Eritrean people took up arms and embarked on their just and legitimate armed struggle, not because this was their choice but the world community had denied their case due attention. In the early years, dialogue of any kind was not possible as the Haile Selassie regime with the active collaboration of the United States had built walls of isolation around the Eritrean struggle and was striving to quietly liquidate the armed struggle.

After the fall of Haile Selassie, the Dergue regime made formally declarations about the issue, as a "peaceful solution" to the Eritrean case was one of the main slogans of the people. What the case demands, however, was not empty proclamations and feigned acceptance of the peoples will, but convection and seriousness, which the Dergue lacked. This lack of commitment on the part of the Dergue doomed any-peace efforts and the peace maneuvers it carried out when it first seized power ended in total failure.

In 1977-78 fake peace talks concocted by the Soviets and directly by the East Germans were conducted as a pretext for the eminent large-scale offensive of the Dergue. A collateral objective of the peace maneuvers was to secure the submission of the Eritrean revolution through deception and intimidation. Four successive meetings were held at the invitation of the German Socialist Workers Unity Party. The first from 25-23/03/77 and the fourth from 09-10-/06/78. On 15/07/78, a month after meeting, the Dergue launched its first large-scale offensive.

At the first meeting held between the EPLF delegation and leaders of the Socialist Workers Unity Party of the German Democratic Republic (East Germany), the latter submitted the following deception opinion.

We affirm the right of the Eritrean peoples to self-determination up to independence, and the Dergue has also assured us that it believes in this right. There are some in the Dergue, however, who do not accept it. talks should, therefore, start to resolve the case. The EPLF delegation gave this initiative its positive consideration and took the opportunity to elaborate on the just and legitimate nature of the Eritrean case, and assured the German side that the EPLF's commitment to peaceful solution and its readiness to start dialogue. A date was set for the next meeting.

Ninth Part

In the second meeting, the German authorities retreated from their previous opinion, informed the EPLF delegates of the presence of a Dergue delegation in Berlin and stated that it has assured them of its readiness to meet with the EPLF delegation. The EPLF delegation proposed that since the East German authorities were aware of EPLF position, they should also get the opinion of the Dergue's delegation and act as mediators between the two groups. The EPLF put forward this suggestion because it wanted to rind out if the Dergue really had a new proposal as the East German had claimed. On their part the Germans proposed face to face talks, and the EPLF agreed. But contrary to the assurance and statement of the Germans, the Dergue did not have a new proposal. In the meeting the delegation of the Dergue launched into a spiel on the 3000 year old history of Ethiopia, the place of Eritrea in that history, the role of the Eritrean revolution in the downfall of Haile Selassie, the Dergue's "program of Democratic Revolution" and the purported gains achieved by the people on basis of the program. The EPLF delegation stated that the myth of a 3000 year old history was specious and baseless, elaborated on the history and the just and legitimate struggle of the Eritrean people and expressed the EPLF's rejection of the Dergue's case. In addition it asked the Dergue's delegation to present its proposal if it had any.

In the third meeting as well, no new proposal was submitted. The EPLF delegation declared that it would present its overall views on the issues. The German representatives presented a four point proposal dealing, in general terms, with continuation of the dialogue and proposed that this should be studied by the two parties, the EPLF and the Dergue. The meeting was concluded after it set a date meeting.

In the fourth meeting, the EPLF delegation handed to the East German authorities a memorandum clarifying historical facts and outlining its clear position on a peaceful solution. It declared that there was nothing to warrant a meeting with the Dergue delegation. However, as the German representatives suggested that the EPLF delegation also hand the document to the Dergue delegation and listen to what ever opinion it may have, a meeting was held and the memorandum given to the representative of the Dergue. When the delegation of the Dergue made a speech with a new and threatening tone, the EPLF delegation declared that the EPLF would, under no circumstance submit to threats and intimidations. The Germans too changed their tone and instead of their usual assurance, warned that the Dergue which had already defeated Somalia, had made massive military preparations, and advised that there would be dire and terrible consequence unless the EPLF changes its stand. They also stated that they would give their opinion on the EPLF memorandum after studying it and would set and announce the date for the next meeting. A month later, the Dergue started its large-scale offensive.

The Berlin meeting were taken by many parties as an opportunity to conduct a propaganda campaign against the EPLF and exploit the difference inside the Eritrean revolution, particularly that between the EPLF and ELF. Although the EPLF had every right to independently initiate, conduct or engage in contacts, it decided to act in coordination with the ELF, because it was determined to ensure that the contacts would not be exploited as a pretext for worsening the internal conflict.

But the EPLF's proposal for a joint and coordinated move was not accepted by the ELF, which was only too eager to misconstrue the talks as having been prompted by the EPLF weakness and intensify the old defamation campaign of EPLF "collusion with the enemy". The Soviet Union too attempted to exploit the Berlin meetings, by directing through various means, an anti-EPLF propaganda campaign and more importantly by making numerous approaches and showing favor to the ELF in an effort in winning the organization.

Tenth Part

The Dergue too went on the propaganda offensive, to accompany its large-scale military campaign professing to have made a serious for peace and alleging to have been re buffed by the EPLF. Confident of quick military victory, the regime, after the Berlin talks did not consider using peace as a maneuver chip. Meanwhile, the Numeiri regime in the Sudan, which had earlier (at Free town, Sierra Leone) and for purpose of its own expressed support of the Eritrean Peoples cause change its stance, offered to mediate and started exerting pressure on the Eritrean revolution to induce it to compromise. Taking in to consideration the effort of the Sudan and other interested parties to organize negotiations, and more importantly, assessing the experiences of Berlin, the EPLF issued its

Referendum Proposal on November 23, 1980 in which it set, in unequivocal terms, its views on a peaceful solution of the Eritrean case, moreover, the EPLF continued with unflagging seriousness its intensive political and diplomatic works in search for sincere dialogue.

Furthermore, governments, organizations and individuals continued to take initiatives for a peaceful solution, initiative to which the EPLF gave positive considerations and whole-hearted support. But the Dergue was not interested. It was only after the debacle of the "Red Star Campaign" that the regime signaled through its agents abroad, its willingness to meet with the EPLF. In its approaches, the Dergue insisted that the meetings be conducted in secret and without the presence of a third party. The EPLF agreed and first meeting was held on 23-08-82. Successive meetings followed on 11-11-82, 03-01-83, 18-02-83, 16-31/5/83, 19-07-

83; 26-12-83, 02-03-84, 31-85......... In all there were ten exploratory meetings.

At first, the secrecy of the meetings was the main point of contention. The EPLF proposed that the meetings be formally declared, that a third party acceptable to both sides participate, and that each side submit its own proposal or work paper. The Dergue did not present any proposal but limited itself to repeating its desire of keeping the meeting secret. With respect to the issue of a third party, the Dergue, at first, emphatically rejected the idea and when it finally relented, it kept insisting on the third party being from those whose views are identical with its own and were thus sure to side with it. By the time the preliminary talks broke down, agreement had not been reached on the matter. In regard to the presentation of position papers that would serve as a basis for dialogue the EPLF submitted the points of its referendum proposal. In contrast, although the Dergue after considerable delay presented a paper similar in content to its regional autonomy proposal, it subsequently declared that the paper did not reflect its final position. This meant that the Dergue had failed to submit a paper incorporating its views. In this situation, the EPLF insisted that the regime present a definite position even if it is one that is not incorporated in the three option of the Referendum Proposal. The representatives of the regime, however, engaged in a maneuver to buy time, as they found it impossible to present a position paper, and to this end requested and were given a clarification on the EPLF's interpretation of the points in the Referendum Proposal. In addition, they kept taking contradictory stands in formal and informal meetings and concentrated their efforts on prolonging or pushing the dates of the meetings. When all the issues pertinent to the preliminary meetings were exhausted, the EPLF took up the basic question once again and proposed that the proper negotiation should start in the form of formally declared meeting with the participation of a mutually agreeable third party when this too rejected the preliminary meetings reached a dead end and was terminated.

Eleven Part

Before the talks had broken dawn, peace initiatives advanced by other parties multiplied and gained wider support presenting the Dergue with a new challenge. On numerous occasions, many governments and organizations called on the Dergue to resolve the issue through peaceful means. To alley the pressure, the Dergue replied that it was already there by meeting with the EPLF, by divulging the preliminary talks which it had insisted should be kept secret and to which it paid lip service. This, in itself, was a bone of contention in the preliminary talks. Even then, the Dergue did not desist from exploiting the meetings for this purpose, while at the same time denying that it was violating the confidentiality of the talks. Internally, the Dergue which had trumpeted each of its offensive as the "final solution", changed its tune, professed interest in peace, and used the preliminary meetings as an opportune expedient to silence the internal criticism of those who were opposed to the war and those who waited to exploit the failure of the 6th offensive. The maneuverings of the regime came to an end only when the EPLF formally disclosed that preliminary talks had taken place but had reached a dead-end as a result of the Dergue's obduracy.

The EPLF's enthusiasm for a just and peaceful political solution has not been dampened by the failure of the preliminary talks. The EPLF has been conducting serious and extensive campaigns for a peaceful resolution of the conflict on the international stage. At the time when the drought was worsening the misery of the peoples of Eritrea and Ethiopia, the EPLF pointed out that the main problem was not drought but war, and that peace would ultimately aid in the control of future natural calamities. Moreover, it reiterated its desire for a peaceful solution and called for a ceasefire and the free passage of relief goods. Although this too was rejected by the Dergue, the interest shown by governments, organizations and individuals towards a peaceful solution did not decline but has steadily increased. One example was the peace initiative undertaken by the Sudanese government and frustrated by the Dergue. Consequently, the EPLF's peace proposal and efforts won wide support in different corners of the globe but the efforts of other parties for peace were more organized and extensive.

Strategic Withdrawal and the Second Congress options for Military Development

Military developments registered between the strategic withdrawal and the second congress is categorized in three stages.

The First Stage

The first stage includes the period the first to the fourth offensives. As previously mentioned, the strategic withdrawal of EPLF forces was in July 1978, and the first offensive continued until the end of August. In this offensive, EPLF forces withdraw from their fronts South of Asmara and North of Embaderho village. The Second offensive started in

December 20 of 1978 and continued till the end of the month, during this time the Front withdrew from its East and South Keren fronts.

The third offensive was held from January 1979 to February 9, 1979 in the fronts of Anseba, Mai'emedo, and North Sahle and around Nakfa-Denden. In the following months of March and April were the fourth offensive allegedly aimed to destroy the North Sahel and Nakfa fronts but those latter attempts were ended in utter failure. During those four offensives, the EPLF forces fought with great determination and patriotism. During those times the front was not only engaged in defending, it also had launched various attacks in places under enemy control.

On those four consecutive offensives the loss of enemy forces was around 25 thousand of its soldiers. Although, it reduced the speed of the attacks, the enemy was still eager to conduct another larger offensive.

The Second Stage

The second stage includes the successive attacks launched on July 8, 1979 that continued to the end of the month, this is the fifth offensive. During this invasion, enemy forces lost 12 thousands of their soldiers and faced huge amount of material loss. The offensive ended up with the defeat of the enemy forces with a huge victory to EPLF forces and had the big psychological and moral effect on the enemy forces. Victories of the fifth offensive also gave a moral boost to EPLF forces to launching further attacks against enemy forces; as a result the first attack was launched in Nakfa in December of 1979. EPLF forces also launched another attack in the Northern Sahel frontier, the outcome of those two attacks were huge that the enemy forces were heavily defeated losing around 15 thousand soldiers. Enemy forces were also forced to withdraw to their base in Afabet, to the lowlands. This victory was not only a success in the military sector, but it also conveyed a message to many that believed the strategic withdrawal was the end of the Eritrean People armed struggle for independence.

Despite the fact that the Derg regime was heavily defeated in the five invasions it launched, it still took a substantial amount of time to prepare itself with armaments and human resources for another big offensive, the sixth offensive, "Keyih Kokob". As part of this latter invasion, the regime deployed thousand of special trained soldiers with various sophisticated weaponry and armament. The invasion was different than the previous invasions because this time the regime was determined to end the Eritrean people struggle for liberation. A number of seminars and meetings were held all over the country including in other parts of the world in a bid to persuade other parties that the invasion has the support of the Eritrean and Ethiopian people. It also issued development programs that seem to benefit the people of Eritrea and various propaganda campaigns were launched. As a result, every one was eager to see the outcomes of the war.

The sixth invasion also is known as the "Wefri Keiyh Kokob" started in February 15, 1982 and continued for ninety- five days. This was one of the severe wars and was followed with some small skirmishes until it ended with total defeat of the regime. The invasion ended with the victory of the EPLF, and the regime lost around 40 thousand of its soldiers and surrendered large number of its weaponry deployed in the country during the invasion.

The sixth invasion also played vital contribution in the history of Eritrean people struggle for independence because starting from the 1979 attack in Nakfa and Northern Sahel frontiers, the Derg regime was having a number of preparations to end the struggle once and for all. As a result, it was launching continuous attacks for two years until the beginning of the sixth invasion which made the EPLF forces be engaged in a continuous defense wars. The victory achieved from the six invasions assured the existence of the struggle and the front.

After the strategic withdrawal ELF were moved to be stationed in the lower part of the Barka region, and the third unit also known as "Sabe's Unit" was also stationed in the lower Barka region. Being stationed in the place where the ELF was first established and having the support of majority of the inhabitants didn't make the ELF happy, and as a result ELF forces begun launching attacks against the third unit until it withdraw to areas bordering the Sudan.

Meanwhile, violating previous agreements the ELF leadership begun to takeout soldiers from their deployment station of joint frontier and this were a huge betrayal because it was a tough time to the EPLF, this took place in 1980.

Before the aforementioned betrayal, they also had begun to attack EPLF forces in Denakalia and in a number of other places. After withdrawing ELF soldiers from the joint frontier the front begun to officially launch attacks against EPLF forces. And until 1981 there was a severe civil war between the two fronts and in 1981 ELF forces fled to Sudan and divided into a number of small units.

The dismantlement of the ELF was a huge lose to the armed struggle, and was a great disappointment to many Eritreans and other sympathizers of the Eritrean people struggle for independence. The incident happening at the times where enemy forces were doing their level best to destroy the struggle for liberation makes the situation worse. Despite this fact the dismantlement of the ELF was a blessing in disguise, since it was the ELF leadership that causes most of the problem and hindrances in the struggle the dismantlement was a solution to many of the problems. It also played vital role in diverting the attention of the struggle be concentrated on the struggle for liberation only. As a result, the sixth offensive launched by the Derg regime was completed with the victory of the EPLF forces.

This latter victory has huge impact on the moral and determination of the people of the country and the fighters, in addition to determining the existence of the struggle, and assurance that no force will defeat the struggle for liberation easily.

The Derg regime that is unable to accept the huge defeat on the sixth offensive begun to prepare for another huge offensive in secret. Meanwhile it also continues to maneuver ploys among the people of the country where they would fight each other. Many Eritrean youth were forced to join the regime where they would fight their own brothers, and as a consequence of those latter actions, EPLF announced a national rebuff campaign, this enable the youth of the country join the struggle for liberation and make their due contribution to the country and the people.

After the Derg finished all the necessary preparation for another attack secretly, it launched an attack on

March 1983 believing that the EPLF forces are weaken from the sixth offensive. Unlike previous attacks, this latest attack was done without any campaigns or any media propaganda, it continued till the mid of August 1983 again ended in utter failure. The Derg lost around 25 thousand soldiers in this offensive only, the huge human and material lose the regime faced in this offensive added to previous loses weakened the power of the regime.

After those continues attacks and the victories achieved, EPLF was transformed to stage where it can launch attacks against the Derg, and this stage was begun with the attacks that liberated of the towns of Aligider and Tessenei in January 1984. Later in February the front launched another attack in the Northern Sahel Frontier, the soldiers of the Derg regime has been deployed in the area for about five years. The attack also known as "Wekaw Eze" continued until March, and in the war from March 19-21, the front defeated the force in the area once and for all. Here there were around 7 thousand soldiers of the regime dead, and 4/5 of the armament and weaponry surrendered.

Two months after this successful attack, the operation that burned 33 Derg airplanes in the capital took place.

Continuing its attacks, EPLF launched several acute attacks in western part of the country that were under the full control of the enemy forces. As part of these attacks, in July 5, 1985 EPLF launched an attack on the town of Barentu and defeated the huge force deployed in the town. Unable to accept its defeat, the Derg regime gathered all its soldiers from all over the country including those deployed in Ogaden and launched counter-attacks until August 26, 1885 where it recaptured the towns of Barentu, Tessenei and Aligidier. The battle of Barentu did slow down the pace of the EPLF attacks but still damage was done to enemy forces where it lost thousands of its soldiers.

After the battle of Barentu, enemy forces launched another attack known as the Bahri Negash Invasion on October 10, 1985. Believing that this was this would be the one and last attack that was going to destroy the struggle, the regime launched huge force with heavy armaments. But these latter attacks were ended in utter failure in December 4, 1985 where the enemy lost around 17 thousand of its soldiers.

In 1986 the regime was unable to launch attacks, in the contrary EPLF was registering huge victories along with the previous attacks in areas fully controlled by enemy, and the ambush and commando operations underway in various parts of the country which makes the victories of front remarkable.

During the time from the strategic retreat to the second congressional meeting, March 1987, there were a number of military conflicts that make clear two important things in the struggle of the Eritrean People to liberation.

First, it made clear that the Derg regime is not going to solve the inquiry of the Eritrean people to liberation peacefully. Despite the fact, that Ethiopia was under a constant drought and famine the regime was engaged in buying various armaments and weaponries to destroy the armed struggle of the Eritrean people. And still the regime was unable to defeat EPLF and was facing huge military and political loses. In contrary to the reality, the former Soviet Union continues to extend its assistance to support the regime.

Second, the long and bitter battles make clear the existence of EPLF and the armed struggle. The latest victories of the battle elucidates the inquiry of the Eritrean people for liberation can't be destroyed through force and that EPLF will fight until the liberation of the people and the country accomplished.

Military planning that out-maneuvered enemy military elites

Afabet located on a vast plain is surrounded with mountains which are interlinked with each other and with very few exists and one who has the capacity to block the exits would have the upper hand. That's what exactly happened during the battle to liquidate the 'mighty' Nadew Command and liberate Afabet. Case in point is the closure of the strategic exits of Adshurum and Kisad-Meshalit by the liberation fighters.

Nadew Command was a strong command formed with 20 thousands foot soldiers, one mechanized brigade, ten battalions as well experienced military commanders, coupled with Soviet military and intelligence advisers. It was also equipped with advanced military hardware including rocket propeller launchers (what we call Stalin Organ), several tanks and cannons of different millimeters and intelligence and surveillance equipment.

With the position they held (13x13 kilometers stretched trenches), with the military hardware they possess and with the advice they were receiving from the Soviet advisors both militarily and intelligence wise they never expected any one force will penetrate their position and do harm to them. Nadew Command for them was indomitable force that could undo any attempt by any force and in fact if it happened it was for its final doom. That was Nadew Command to the Derge regime. And it stayed there for 10 years consolidating its power by the day.

What the commanders of the Derge regime and its Soviet advisers didn't realize was that Eritrea is of its people and the EPLF commanders as sons and daughter of Eritrea know their country from its in and out. They know the location of every mountain, hill and valley. And above all they had people ready to cooperate on what they are asked at any one time and place for they were also part liberation army from behind the front line and in the middle of the enemy forces.

The EPLF military commanders had accumulated the necessary experience during the long years of combat and had well studies the mentality and psychological make up of the enemy. They well know how to create panic on the part of the regime and take advantage of it. To give some instances before the operation to liquidate the Nadew Command:

52nd Division of the EPLF walked on foot 16 hours behind the front line to reach Kisad-Meshalit unnoticed by the enemy. It went all the way from around Areza, Mai-Dima (both located in Southern region), Golij (Gash Barka region) through Elaberd, Keren (Anseba region) to Kisad-Meshalit. Division 13 had to walk on foot through Mai-Aini, Dekemhare, Segeneity to reach its destination. The Derge regime was expecting that Division 52 to attach Keren and Division 13 Dekemhare or Segeneity. But that all military maneuvers were to divert the attention of the Derge commanders and create panic on them. The sole purpose for walking all through was to divert the attention of the Derge regime. And sometimes all communications are halted and the enemy become black out on what is happening and where these Divisions are heading for. And that was exactly what happened.

The power of EPLF besides the morale of its combatants was the capacity of its intelligence units. The intelligence units were very much familiar with the terrain and psychological make-up of the enemy. They used to penetrate the enemy line at will and they played a great role in the operation to liquidate the command.

The operation for the demise of the Nadew Command began on March 17 with all fronts. On the second day of the operation a large enemy military hardware was blocked at Adshurm. Adshurum was the only gate way fro the running enemy soldiers and their equipment to reach Afabet. The leading tank on the run was hit at Adshurum and all the rest had no way to escape except wait and see the final demise of it. The enemy understanding that there is no way out with blocked of the only route for escape resorted to destroying its military hardware by aerial bombardment and many fall in the hands of the liberation fighter for later use in the struggle for independence.

At the opposite site Division 52 was stationed at Kisad-Meshalit with two missions. One was to block and kill the reinforcement that could come from Keren area and the other mission to deny exit to the fleeing soldiers from Afabet. And here the fleeing soldiers of the Derge had no way to go through and reach Keren except accepting their due: death or surrender.

The operation for demise of Nadew Command and the liberation of Afabet was a limestone in the history of the struggle for liberation and out-maneuvering the intelligence of the Ethiopian military elites and the Soviet advisors. From that it was only a question of time for the total independence of Eritrea and the coming true the aspiration of the Eritrean people.

The successive offensives and liberation of Eritrea

Almost two years after the demolition of Nadow Iz, continuous large scale military operations were conducted in a bid for the EPLF to preserve the victories already obtained and transcend into new military offensives while the Derg regime to avoid further military loses and regain what it had already lost. Though the EPLF conducted large scale military operation in April 1988 in the Keren front in a bid to preserve the momentum of Nadew Operation the outcome was not successful as expected. It again launched another offensive in May and again did not materialize. The Derg military after they felt seemingly consolidating their stronghold at the Keren front after suffering heavy lose; they established a new front at the plains of Azhara and

Maemide to avoid the pressure coming from the EPLF and to take back Afabet. The huge military attempts were met with strong resistance and they suffered again a heavy lose. More over, the EPLF forces conducted tactical attack and rearranging of position at the Mensae front and with that the initiative of the enemy was was doomed to failure. The military development during the second half of 1988 was the offensive of the EPLF navy at the Massawa archipelago and its environs. Though the EPLF Navy was with limited capacity its role in the military operations and its future development as an important force was understandable. Within 10 months of the year 1988 around 45 thousand of the Derg manpower was out of action.

All possibilities that were initiated by the enemy through the Keren front were blocked. With that the concentration of the EPLF shifted towards the east plains, and in the beginning of 1989 it conducted successful mechanized offensive at the northern plains of Semhar; the successful Shire operation together with the Ethiopian People's Revolutionary Democratic Front (EPRDF); and in 1989 the victorious Assosa operation. These all successful operations inside Eritrea and Ethiopia not only were important military and political developments but also were gate ways to the historical Fenkil Operation. Until the Operation Fenkil 50 small and big scale military operations were conducted.

From 08 to 01, 1990, the historic Fenkil Operation was conducted that liberated Massawa and cut the road from Massawa to Ghindae. The operation was special in all aspects. It was also an operation which killed the morale of the enemy and the binging of the end of its stay in Eritrea. The international community also forced to believe the eminent independence of Eritrea. In the combats conducted within two years including those 14 combats conducted at the end of 1990, in 64 combats the Derg regime lost 110 thousand of its forces.

The different attempts by the EPLF at Bizen prior to the Fenkil Operation to rearrange position and to set conducive ground for future programs were not successful. The enemy was so anxious that it was compelled to from February 1990 to conduct successive attempts in the Ghinda environs and Northern Red Sea. On the part of the EPLF it understood that the chance of penetrating the Ghinda front was minimal but to consolidate position. And in the end of April 1990 launched the southern offensive and within one month it liberated Senafe, Adi-Keih and Segeneity. The enemy to retaliate loses it encountered at the south fronts launched heavy failed offensives in the Bizen, Ghinda and Girat Awli'e. The offensive of the EPLF in September 1990 to liberate Dekemkare was not successful. And the two offensives conducted in March of the same year in the eastern and southern Asmara aimed at increasing the pressure on the Derg that was very much worried of its shrinking logistics and aerial support was not yet successful.

The offensive of the enemy in 1990 at the Halhal front was also foiled.

After the successive offensives and counter offensives conducted for a year long, in order to enter into the last and concluding offensive the EPLF conducted heavy offensive in March at the Tio, Idi and as well as at Assab environs and at same time in 19/05/91 launched another heavy offensive at the Dekemhare front that ended with the liberation of Asmara in 24/05/1991. The 130,000 enemy forces that were stationed in Eritrea were defeated. The TPLF offensives that were being conducted inside Ethiopia have also to be equally remembered. With that the EPLF accomplished its mission of liberating the country from the yokes of colonialism.

Culture

Wedding Tradition
A Glimpse into a Traditional Afar Wedding

Eritrea is a nation endowed with multi ethnic groups, different languages and cultures living in peace and harmony, each practicing its own different traditional customs. Among these diverse practices is the traditional wedding customs of the Afar ethnic group. There are three ways of planning a wedding in Afar ethnic group which is mostly similar to different other ethnic groups in the country. Sometimes the parents agree for marriage when a child is born and the male's family chooses a bride and it grows solely by the choice of the man.

The first thing the groom does is after he chooses a bride is informing his father and ask for his approval. Because his father could not only decide his son's wedding, he calls his brothers and then the approval of the wedding is discussed within the group discussions. During these discussions, the father consults his son's choice and asks if the girl is suitable. The uncles also discuss where and which family the bride is from. If the family is a distant, one of the groom's uncles suggests it'd be better if the groom would take his daughter. After long and exhaustive discussions, the groom is asked again about the offer. But since a man can not be deprived of his choice in this culture, he gets his approval from his father and his uncles.

The men give their blessings and pray for the fulfillment of their thoughts. Since the groom's family has discussed in approving the wedding, what comes next is informing the bride's family. Then the family of the groom's father head to the bride's residence.

After welcoming the guests, the bride's father schedules the meeting between the two sides in order to discuss the issues with the uncles of the girl and his clan. In Afar, the clan is informed as a tradition. But most of the time the decision of the wedding relies on the uncles of the girl.

More than the father, the uncles and the girl's family play a key role when it comes to the approval of the wedding. It is after the approval of the uncles that the mother of the girl goes and tells her daughter that she is going to get married. At this point of time, both the families gather and decide the schedules for the time of the wedding.

After the first step is done, both fathers of the bride and the groom proceed to the administrator of the village in Afar to the Derder or Sultan of the city. The wedding is then officially approved and both sides of the families finalize their legal duties.

It is after this that the exact timing of the wedding is being decided. The wedding could be after several months or even a year. The men then depart after praying for the success of the wedding.

Three days before the wedding, there is a special ceremony prepared by women of the village. Bookali, which is an ornament scented with butter and different perfumed leaves, is prepared on this occasion so the bride could put it on during her wedding day.

Different programs are prepared for the ceremony. They dig a small hole and put their container made of clay in the hole for three days. This specific norm has passed through generations; it's believed to be a good omen for the weeding if the women who participate in the making of the perfume butter for the bride are still married. That way the smell of the perfume butter is believed to be stronger so that the bride could put it on her body on the wedding day.

The women are dancing different songs praising the girl and her family.

During this ceremony the mother of the girl breeds the girl in two or three corner and the girl hides in her friend's house. She hides there for four to five days before the wedding. The girl occasionally comes to her house covered in order to assist her mother with in the household. The reason why the girl hides is to avoid exposure to different invitees for the different ceremonies even before the wedding day.

The girl returns to her bed room just two days before the wedding day along with her friends and her friends sing different songs for her. After this, a man comes to the girl and moves her to the left and right as a sign of testing the girl's endurance. This tradition is known as Niksow.

The girl could not stand from where she fell the whole day until her friends come in the afternoon to help her prepare for the wedding. The person who does her hair for the wedding should also be someone who is married.

The eve of the wedding is then celebrated in the house of the Derder or the Sultan. The villagers then make for the beginning of signal of the Derder at dawn by the Banda to precede the wedding ceremony.

Everyone then goes and gathers in the house of the Sultan Abdelqadir Dawd which is beautifully decorated by the women in the village. This gathering is to handle occasions to the members of Feima. With in the Feima, all the members of the legislation above the age of 15 which serve as the main assistance of the Derder in the rules and regulations of the Sultanate.

It is mandatory that the Feima is informed about any wedding ceremony in the villages just a day before. The Feima then officially decides if the wedding is going to be held or not. They could ban the wedding if the father of the bride or groom has been convicted of any crime or did not abide by the legislation of the Sultanate; and in such case, the Feima sees to it that the proper punishment is imposed upon the families.

This wedding has already been approved by the Feima. So both the families are only waiting for the signal to begin the wedding ceremony. At this time the groom chooses two of his best men and the head of the Feima chooses two for the groom's best men during the wedding.

The Dekar, a traditional drum is played for the honor of the groom and elders are presented with different food provided by the groom's family.

The women wearing glittering clothes with their silvers, gold as well as other decorations on their hair, play and dance until dusk. Different traditional dances such as Denkalit and Malebuwa are performed during this time.

On the groom's side, one of the best men gives the groom a hair cut and prepares a head of washing his body. The groom also washes his hair with an egg after a hair cut. One of his trusted men encloses the groom and ties a stick on his hand, known as the Ketel, which is not allowed to put it on the ground. After this, the groom goes out to eat a special food prepared by his mother-in-law. The special food is known as Ara-Iskwada, which is made of milk, butter, rise and different spices.

It is said that this food is specially prepared for the strength of the groom and nobody starts to eat before he does. The groom is said to be even above his father forty days after he's washed with Henna. Similarly, the bride prepares for the wedding while her hair is being breaded while different plays and dances are taking place.

The perfume butter prepared and buried in the hole for three days is opened and put in different containers on the wedding day.

The honeymoon house among the Afar ethnic group, which is called Ado Ari (afar for white house) is prepared by the bride's family. It is chosen to be further away from the main house of the bride. Therefore, the villagers gather to help build the house after a message is sent early in the morning through the Banda, already made of antelope's horn.

The bride's mother usually accompanies the couple to help them construct their house and returns home after three days. When the wife gets pregnant, the husband usually takes her back to her family for delivery. The husband would then dismantle the mat house.

What Happens After the Wedding?

Soon after the rainy season, which we have had abundantly this year, there comes the harvesting season. And just before farmers get their hands full with all of the, tough but, happy field work to fill-up reaped crop enough to cover the family's table for the whole year and much for stores in town to be sold, this time of the year is moreover traditionally scheduled for weddings; a rather relaxed time of merriments, joy and, the 'can't do without', typical and lovely festivities that don't deny dancing.

Therefore, now is the time of festivities and Asmara's parks are busy hosting couples wedding photos.

My cousin Mike got married to his lovely girl Honey a couple of weeks ago, and I have had, the blessing to directly be part of a blend of beautiful tradition that I am honored to share with you.

The rainbow of cultural practices seen throughout a wedding are numerous, especially when in Eritrea we have nine ethnic groups each with myriad of flamboyant customs. So much so, a whole book, would not be enough. What I will be zooming in on though, is the after marriage activities, of which I was part of in my cousin's wedding, coated up by some research I did prompted by its radiance. Henceforth, some facts about local honeymoons.

The meaning of marriage in Eritrea, goes way far from just the bringing of two people in the holy sense of matrimony. It actually penetrates all the way to its holistic version of merging two families, two communities, two hometowns and two holy kinship lines. Which is exactly why, when a couple decides to get married, the first ones to know after the couple itself: are the parents. The parents will then tell the elders and later the elders, of both side, would start their mission towards the making of this blessed merger.

Aren't we just well raised children?! ... We let parents meddle with 'our' stuff even at the age of thirty!!!

Looking up for some common ascent in the lineages, for example is one of their technical mission, in doing so the families give thanks to that ascent for allowing 'the joint'. Elders believe, we Eritreans are of 'a' family: they do not discriminate at all. In fact, truth be told, the furthest the lineage the better, because not only are they happy to merge two families but also –and here comes a common saying we hear a lot: "megeshi yikonena", meaning an excuse for a holiday trip to visit a, geographically distant but emotionally, close family. (Wow! how awesome are they?!).

And at the end, the wedding happens with the blessing of the community, and things get even a lot more exciting afterwards.

Conventionally, even if a couple is to live on its own, it does not happen immediately after. The couple heads straight to the groom's house for honeymoon; in Tigrigna it's called 'hitsnot'. The groom's family has the duty of decorating the newlyweds' room, and for as long as a month or more, the bride and the groom are treated like royalty. In fact even their title is promoted to His and Her Royalty, 'Goytay' and 'Imbeytey' in Tigrigna. I am not ridiculing; one cannot just have the audacity to call them less! It's traditionally wrong, and punishable by money for entertainment purposes.

The newlywed couple is not allowed to go out of the house, so friends and family are those to visit instead. During these godly weeks of a super relaxed honeymoon, all there is to do for His and Her Highness is simply: sleeping, prettying-up under constant facial, body and, you name it anything else care, hanging out with friends and family, eating tons of delicious food without having to go to the kitchen and watch and re-watch over and over again the wedding videos; and more likely make fun of those who dance weird. In few words: heaven!

The groom's family is the busiest after the Sunday wedding ceremony. For an unlimited time of the honeymoon season, they are obliged to prepare refined catering from breakfast all the way to dinner, not only for the bride and groom, but also for the hundreds of visitors that come regularly by to congratulate the newlywed couple.

Free dinner and free drinks! It is the groom's family greatest pleasure for as many visitors as possible. Also, you don't visit just once, you can go every day. For a while, if a friend is married, the groom's house would be the new hangout spot.

Mostly, the most hectic visiting hours are after seven in the evening. The living room gets overly crowded. That is the common schedule for the youth to hang out and party with His and Her Royalty. First dinner is served and then alcohol-ed up drinks follow: Siwa, Scotch and more. Endless chats, laughter, dances and tons of fun games. The newlywed would be left alone only after one or two AM at night.

Talking about games for example, the games usually played during honeymoons are table games, such as 'Gebeta' a traditional game similar to chess but with small marbles. There is also 'Sheded' and this one is an extremely loved one. The game is played with six or more sticks and it is a truth or dare game. All of the people involved in the game take turn to flip the sticks and catch as many as possible. If one is not able to catch as much as the decided number, the best man, wedges the player's left hand between the sticks and asks for questions or dares. He keeps baffling the poor left hand until the truth is told, or the dare executed.

Moreover, Vegas is also brought to the newlywed's room. Ladies and Gentlemen I am talking about card games and bets! Cash is allowed! In fact, despite the fact that bet is illegal in the country, even the courthouse goes easy for these delightful events.

The game of cards might have evolved with time, but it goes years back. The young ladies and gentlemen love to play cards, and the cash put on stake can reach multiple of thousands. The bettors hate to lose, so the game only naturally gets intense. So much so, that by the end of the night the ladies give up and sit in a group whining of boys and boy's attitudes. However, here comes the lovely and sweet part of the game; when the boys end being boys, the accumulated thousands of cash is given to the newlywed. Darling right? ... A token of appreciation from friends, with an intent to assist the newlywed couple with some start-up cash for future endeavors.

The food provided is all traditional: tsebhi dorho, fresh enjera every day and just many and many more traditional delicacies. There is a regulation though; the mother in law does not allow left over. In fact, three days after my cousin's wedding, I noticed how my auntie refused to cook more for following days unless we finish everything on the table. Meaning, all the provided ration has to vanish. Henceforth, what the youngsters do is to wipe the plates, play a little game called 'Akualalas'. The best man decided on a spontaneous rule, 'don't laugh', for example. Unless of course you want to be a direct witness of stomach explosion, then you'd better resist laughing, as everybody starts acting weird;

like zombies. You have no idea how sidesplitting and quirky it can get when grownups act weird! So definitely not an easy task. Whoever laughs gets a spoonful from every one sitting on the table!

Speaking of rules, the couple has also the right of decreeing a set of regulation. They print it and post it on the wall for everyone to see and abide by. These rules are light hearted instruction, totally aimed at making fool of visiting friends and family, if one does not adhere to them, then better cash out his/her change.

After the weeding on Sunday, that next Thursday is exceptionally special for the bride. And that is because that afternoon she receives some very special guests: her family! After spending so much time with the groom, his family and friends, Thursday evening is particularly reserved for her mother, sisters and aunts.

As early in the morning, the bride's family sends to the groom's family tons of himbasha (Tigrigna traditional sweet bread), the ones to deliver are the best man and the maid of honor. Then once the delivery is made, the groom's mother breaks it to slices and sends out as many kids as possible to disseminate the sweet pastry to all the neighbors. It is truly a delight to watch, young adorable children running around like flaying little angels, from door to door, delivering a token of the bride's mother. On Thursday, breakfast for neighbors is provided by the bride's mother. Also, an act of sharing and giving thanks to the community while rejoicing in the welcoming of a new daughter member.

Meanwhile, before actually going out to see her family for the first time in days, it's a storm of butterflies on Her Highnesses' belly. Honey; my new sister in law, literally turned red in the anxiousness of seeing her mother and sisters.

A nerve racking moment of a girl turned wife. A mother daughter emotional reunion.

The bride joins her family accompanied by her husband. She carries with her the most expensive and nicest perfume she has; she sprays some on the guests every time she hugs and kisses someone. This action has two meanings: A. "Don't worry mom, I am doing as beautifully as this perfume" and B. braggingly: "Look at the Channel my husband got me!"

In the afternoon, the bride's family arrives and it's a pleasant family reunion, called 'Hamawuti'.

Actually, all honeymoon long, in a wonderfully ornamented basket the bride puts beautiful nail polishes of her choice, a remover and perfumes as well. In this fashion, every lady whom stops by the honeymoon, has to do some manicure and put on some perfume. It is known that in doing so, the girls share some of the bride's luck. In fact, it is not allowed to wash off the perfume shortly, the girls keep the blessing in their closet for as long as possible.

Like I said before, marriage in Eritrea, is not solely about two people, it is about family, friends and the community at large. Beyond the high possibility of Cupid striking His enchanted arrows between young family members and friends of both parties, and beyond brand new bonds of friendship being created; honeymoons are stunning conventions of venerating the essence of unification through the marriage of two people: honeymoons are an openhearted receptions, where by the creation of a future new-family, is welcomed by the community.

Which is why honeymoons are carefully worked on. Of course, it must be hard to host hundreds of people but the toil is not counted, as Eritreans for better or worse, rejoice being together, value brotherhood, friendship and simply having each other.

Happy honey moon to my cousin Mike and all of my fellow Eritrean newlyweds! We welcome your family!

Romance Perspective

This might seem like a banal topic to discuss but I find it worthy to spill my messy mind into it and say a word or two.

What does romance look like in the 21st century? I have been pondering this question for the last few months; ever since I texted what I thought was a rather lighthearted list of ways a man should treat a lady. To be sure, many of the items on the list were of a romantic nature. Some of my friends found fault with the old-fashioned brand of romance and chivalry I suggested, that the list evoked a nauseatingly romantic, antiquated Prince Charming archetype that promotes dangerous lessons about masculinity (and femininity) and therefore has no place in modern times. These critiques got me to thinking about the construct of romance and its role in current-day relationships.

We inhabit a world in which every aspect of romance from meeting to mating has been streamlined, safety-checked, and emptied of spiritual consequence. The result is that we imagine we live in an erotic century of unprecedented opportunity when, in fact, we live in an erotic century that is almost unendurably bland, romance in today's society has become anemic; it's been bled out of us, replaced by a commodification and demystification, among other things. Romance in our day has become a poor and shrunken thing. To some it remains an explicit embarrassment, a discredited myth, the deceptive sugar that once coated the pill of women's servility. To others, romance has become a recreational sport. As we have lost sight of romance we are no longer able to let it, sweep us up, to take us for a flight in the heavens, a twirl into the unknown.

But what exactly is romance? Can it even be defined in specific terms or is it too personal an experience to be painted in precise strokes?

And the truth is that romance is too personal an experience to define as one way of being or acting toward one another for both men and women, and ultimately an intricate and unique equation for singles and couples alike to decipher.

I'd be remiss if I didn't address the fact that many modern-day creatures still want to perceive and define romance in old-fashioned ways and long for a traditional brand they fear no longer exists, a brand that flourished in bygone eras when the rules to courtship were perhaps clearer, when the act of courting itself was in vogue. I can understand why.

But before that, in traditional Eritrea, love was utterly unheard of. Getting married with some one of your own choosing was frowned upon and considered an embarrassment. Marriages were simply put, arranged by the elderly and respected. Arranged marriages were set in a way that strengthened family bonds between two close families or friends.

In an arranged marriage, the bride and groom were selected by a third party rather than by each other. These marriages were usually set up by the parents or an older family member because of circumstances and conveniences. The match could be selected by parents, or a trusted third party. In many communities, priests or religious leaders as well as relatives or family friends played a major role in matchmaking.

Arranged marriages varied in nature and in how much time elapsed between meeting and engagement. In an "introduction only" arranged marriage, the parents may only introduce their son or daughter to a potential spouse. From that point on, it is up to the children to manage the relationship and make a final choice. There is no set time period.

First, preferences were given to the same background. The ancestry of the individual and the family's culture and traditions also played an important part. Usually, prospective spouses were looked for from families belonging to the same region and having the same language and food habits.

That is until one wit started to have 'feelings' for Tsirha, who fetched water from the Village's Waterwell each morning. He of course couldn't ask her out on a date, which was completely unheard of; instead, he asked her if she could pick lice out of his Afro hair. And that was how they started talking and one too many times of lice picking and talking to each other, they fell in love with one another and decided to tell their parents that they were going to marry each other. Their respective parents of course lost their minds but couldn't change the mind of their supposed to be "in love" children….. Simpler Times!!!!

To older readers, the scenario above may have at least a vague, distant familiarity. But to younger readers, it may be utterly foreign, antiquated and unrealistic—like viewing a scene from an old

Tigrigna film in a world accustomed to the rapid-fire images of a high-definition action movie.

Ultimately though, romance in the 21st century isn't as simple as it should have been, first there is the issue of dating; dating has a long and varied history. Over the decades in the Western world, traditional dating was gradually overtaken by the high school "going steady/boyfriend-girlfriend" approach. Those who did not find a romantic counterpart in this way would then often be initiated into the bar/nightclub scene, where they could hope to find someone who may want to hook-up which could eventually lead to the two parties becoming friends with benefits, boyfriend and girlfriend, or possibly even lead to marriage years down the road.

With the rise of the hook-up culture in the west, has come a change in the overall mentality behind dating. The focus in the 21st century is less about finding someone to date court and marry than finding someone who can be fun "for the moment."

"Raised in the age of so-called 'hookup culture,' millennials—who are reaching an age where they are starting to think about settling down—are subverting the rules of courtship," I once read in The New York Times.

Now what has that got to do with Eritrea's younger generation?

Well, everything!

The negative characteristics that define our generation are most evident in their dating lives, particularly in the establishment of permanent long-lasting relationships, thanks to western influences. In an age where social media plays a great role in one state of development, our generation are simply being brainwashed by what they see on movies and read on explicit books.

The brainwashed generation as I would like to call them, have lost all the meaning there is to romance and love. What is love after all, I don't date, I just hangout, I don't committee, I like being free, they would say, along with so many other callous views towards courtship and romance.

Therefore, games are never ending. Apparently this is very common. Earlier, every person wanted a 'commitment' and today, "label-free" relationship is all they want because it gives them all kinds of freedom. They say a lot more on texts than they'll ever say face-to-face or while talking on the phone (which according to them is useless). The era of conversing face to face is a thing of the past.

Either you end up dating for too long or your relationship ends in a few days. Even if you date for too long, there's a chance that it won't work even after so many years. Hence, you obviously end up believing that you really don't know if the term "love" even exists.

"Breaking up" is a game, they break up every other day for every other reason, so much so that you really don't realize when it's TIME to break up.

In most cases, the break ups happen because one of the two has stopped feeling anything for the other person since he/she is too bored by then. People walk in and out of a

relationship effortlessly. While it may be easy for one person to move on from the person he/ she is dating, the other is left behind crying for days. Well that's the way couples balance their relationships these days.

Guys wait three days before they call a girl they are interested in, and girls are not better either, their time is wasted comparing one guy to the other, which all of the above is shocking for me to hear and see, hence my article, I thought such nonsense only existed on movies and such unintelligent behaviors were simply supposed to be confined to our TV screens and books, and subject to our supposedly critical minds.

Romance is not necessarily about one gender doing and one gender receiving via opened doors or bestowed long-stemmed roses or paid tabs; it's a genderless concept. It's about creating for another human being a feeling of being cared for, admired, special, appreciated, valued, protected even. Sweeping gestures can be great, but the real hope for romance today lives on in the attentive touches and thoughtfulness we bestow upon each other in our day-to-day lives. These things never go out of style, at any phase of a relationship.

However, our generation have become not critical of what they see on TV or what they read on books now days, what they see on western movies have spilled out into their own lives and culture and have encoded the way they love and care for one another. They have become apathetic, with no regard for love, honesty, faithfulness, loyalty towards the other gender. Once upon a time not long ago, our fathers put our mothers in pedestal so high they were proud and our mothers respected our fathers accordingly because that is what our culture is ingrained in.

So is romance dead? Most probably yes, but can it be revived? Definitely.

I truly believe romance in whatever form works for you or another, is a positive force for men and women, the glue that can hold us together through the inevitable confusion that erupts out of our sometimes volcanic differences.

Which leads me to leave you with some sage advice from the shy and inimitable Matthew Cuthbert, who says to his adopted daughter Anne Shirley (an eternal romantic), in Lucy Maud Montgomery's "Anne of Green Gables", "Don't give up all your romance, Anne. A little of it is a good thing – not too much, of course – but keep a little of it, Anne, keep a little of it."

Culture driver for development

Human beings are rooted in cultural systems, molded and constrained by their cultures, and for the most part, act only within the cultural realities of their lives. Development of any kind, be it social, political or economic, requires supportive culture. Political, economic and military performances of a nation are not only highly influenced – potentially even determined – by the existing culture.

The policies and the working culture must be congruent with one another. Policy is said to be effective and operative if it creates harmony with the culture. But this does not mean that government policy should hold the tail of culture. Every culture is not inherently positive and progressive. We should not allow ourselves to be mired in reactionary, conservative and destructive elements of culture. Culture is not a static phenomena; it often involves a continuous process of washing and chopping to remove the unnecessary elements.

Culture is the medium through which individuals express their ability to fulfill themselves and it is therefore an integral part of development. A society without the knowledge of their past history and culture is like a tree without roots. Culture is also a vehicle for economic development, social cohesion and the formation of a modern and competitive political system. A strong national culture characterized by a strong work ethic, wise use of resources, mutual respect, and appreciation of diversity is, above all, the product of progressive culture.

Culture affects the ability of countries to establish and sustain economic and political development. The impact of culture on economic development, either as a stimulus or a constraint is vivid. For example racial or gender-based violence and other forms of discrimination in a society cannot be eliminated without changing the culture. In this case, the diverse culture of Eritrea promotes personal responsibility, discipline and hard work, the value of education, honorable service, devotion to a purpose, and commitment to family and community. At the same time however, there still exist strong cultural and religious elements that often represent obstacles to the enormous efforts made by Eritrean society in the battle against poverty and backwardness. For example, consumerism and consumer culture are quietly, yet steadily, spreading throughout our society. If we continue to act as though the highest fulfillment comes from consumption or that more is inherently "better", it is going to be very hard to realize our goals of development.

Culture affects the economic behavior of the society through different means, such as festivals and celebrations of cultural, national or religious days. Every society has a number of meaningful days and people tend to perform some rituals and even organize activities to celebrate. The problem arises not necessarily in the meanings attached to the day, but to the manner of celebration; quite often within the latter we completely forget the former. Many of our cultural practices like engagement, marriage, graduation ceremony, baptism, due to the spread of consumerism and other factors have grown to be more extravagant and the definition of excessive. Simplicity has been replaced by complexity. Attempts have been made to return the focus of celebrations on their original meanings, but changes are slow. Transforming cultures is of course not an easy task. It will require individuals, communities, government and non-government institutions to work tirelessly to cut the unreasonable association of happiness and consumption.

Celebration may strength our cultural identity but if it overlooks or neglects the issue being celebrated it becomes harmful and can dilute the importance of the event. Moreover, excessive celebration poses socio-economic challenges, including to individual or family savings. Together with a culture of work, there must be a culture of leisure. By all means people need time to relax, to be together with families, to enjoy and play, but not at the cost of their regular income or to the level of falling into considerable debt. The regular income of the general population is relatively low and thus unable to cover vast, extravagant celebrations. Excessive celebrations dilute the meaning of our events, bring neither economic wellbeing nor social betterment to the general population, and we should consider their role in our families or communities.

Globalization, with its ever-increasing social and economic interactions, provides opportunities for development, while also presenting enormous challenges to traditional culture and identity. Culture, in all its forms, is essential to address these global challenges. Institutions of higher education, museums and other institutions working close to culture and society through research and education, have to lead and provide the population with relevant and needed culture and expose the futility of extravagance. We have to develop a culture which satisfies the material and spiritual needs of individuals and communities.

Foreign cultures having nothing to do with our culture and belief are also gaining popularity which encourages wastage. For example, Christmas celebrations and Valentine's Day are gaining popularity, especially within urban areas. Of course, this is not to advocate the refusal of cultural globalization – since it has many great advantages and benefits; rather, what should be challenged, is the blind emulation and worshipping of foreign culture that can dilute our own rich heritage.

Fighting poverty is much harder than fighting an invading army. We can't defeat poverty only through hard work (the latter is necessary condition, but not a solely sufficient one). We have to develop a lifestyle that is compatible to our conditions. We should spend our time and money on only what is necessary (with the understanding that leisure and happiness are also necessary!). Locally, we often describe to persons who are careful with their money as people with "a scorpion in their pocket." For many Eritreans, especially the young generation, frugality and retrenchment is not necessarily a virtue. Many reiterate the Tigrigna proverb nxba'H zbl ayexb'Halu "whosoever saves for tomorrow lest live".

No society has become modern without developing productive and progressive culture. We succeeded in our war for liberation despite the challenging odds because we developed a culture that satisfied the demands of the struggle. Consonance of culture with the objective reality of the society was a key to success. As what has been done during the revolution for independence we need to formulate abstemious and sober culture by adopting positive and useful features and rejecting the bad and harmful aspects. We must develop a culture that promotes saving and investment to support our journey toward individual and community growth and development.

Consumerism works by manufacturing unsatisfied desires in the mind of the people. Time has yet not come for Eritreans with low income to associate happiness and satisfaction with consumption. We have to try to open the many doors to happiness by owning a few keys. For our advantage, we must be savers, investors, and creators, not simply takers and consumers.

Eid Etiquettes

Kulu Amin Wa Antum Bikier, is the first wish and greeting of the day every Muslim exchanges and also would likely hear first thing in the morning, to an instant reply of Kulu Sena Wa Antum Tayubun by others who happen to be relatives or even those passing the streets. That Arabic wish literally is translated as, May you all remain safe every year while the reply goes as, May you all remain well.

A fabulous and well-mannered wishes continue on flowing through out the whole day so all the people feel the joy and harmony of the Eid, having men closed in their white Jelebyas (Arab traditional cloak) and women wearing their colorful Liwyets (traditional women garments) head to the morning Eid prayer glorifying their lord Allahu Akbar ... Allahu Akbar, in a uniform and loud tone of voice.

Eid Al Fitr is one of the major holidays in the Muslim community of the world, where they celebrate and have fun after a blessed fasting month of Ramadan. Eid days are commonly celebrated through various cultural activities that fits the environment and their respective societies of the world. People throughout the world have their own ways of celebrating this beautiful day. First thing to do in the day of Eid is praying the Eid prayer in the morning; that's the main common thing. Faithful offer the Eid prayer gathering in one field that can hold them all.

In the early times here in Asmara city we used to pray in the Jamie Mosque near Merkato in the liberty avenue. But then the number of the praying people exceeded the place and reached down the main streets. Then, it was decided that all the Eid prayers after that moment to be held at the Bahti Meskerem square.

Meanwhile, the other activities that are done after the prayer depend on the cultural habits of the people and their surroundings. Eid Al Fitr in our country is well articulated and massively honored by both the Muslims and Christians. Everyone is held in having the day be at its most, by visiting each other's home and congratulating one another.

As far as I can recall, being a child and attending the day of Eid in such nation of ours colors the day of the child and leaves a lasting memory. If a family takes it fine and hands you over the responsibility of looking after your younger siblings and take them to visit every door, somehow you are a very lucky person in the world.

That very moment you are the Boss of the day, you demand whatever you want, to the younger siblings. Simultaneously, it's a hectic job to do, seeing it now, you are the manager of the day, what an experience before a lesson. Well, I have been doing this for at least three or may be four years, having my younger sisters in both of my hands and taking them to every door of the relatives we knew. But, if all of us are to go for Mieyad (a word derived from Eid meaning to visit the relatives), it's on a condition that should be fulfilled before the day. First thing all of us have to wear NEW, top to bottom. I got to get a new haircut; and my sisters are in the beauty salon early in the morning before I get back from mosque.

New Haircut, New shirts, new trousers, new socks and pair of shoes, All New! Then, all is well, we all march to the long day, eating and drinking sweet. If you got unique chocolates you don't eat them but keep them all till night, so you can eat them slowly feeling the extreme sweetness they hold.

Most of all, what every child expects as treasury of the day becomes the Meeyedi: this is a gift that every child receives from close families while they go for visit. If you save more than ten box that very day, you are like Bill Gates or Tim Cook of the day. It's a lot of money for the child, feeling an urge to be back home and tell mom and dad that so and so gave him or her that amount of money and let them keep it for him or her for later.

Another story, back then when I was an elementary school student, I was as usual, told to take my younger sisters for Mieyad. You know what I refused to do so because I did not get to cut my hair cut, which was supposedly to be carried out by my brother. That only day I stayed at home when everyone was having fun and I got pissed off the whole day. That is how much Eid means to children in this culture of ours.

On the other side, the elders take on visiting each other soon after the Eid prayer. Initially, it is normal to pay a visit to your close family members; your father's house, sisters who got married, brother's, uncles and aunts, grandpas and grandmas, after that the remaining kinfolks get the chance to be visited.

If the visitor is well programmed knowing where and where to go, then the task to finish all of the family remains pretty simple, otherwise like others do it, simply and wisely, just take three days off their job so as they can reach everyone restfully. It depends on how many houses you get to in the day of Eid and on how much the family is interconnected. On the streets all children block your ways asking in demand Meeyedi... Meeyedi so you can give them from the sweets you received, they are really the flavor of the day.

A common recipes of the Eid day, and that everybody don't want to miss is the Aba'eke drink. It is sweet and healthy drink, were everybody in the society regardless the faith wants to have. To my understanding, it is fermented not more than a week before the Eid day. Its taste varies according to how Wehale or "Effective" the mother is on the process of fermentation. My mom is one of the Wehale ones, because we never ceased to drink the Aba'eke up until it becomes filter. The other unique recipes of the day are the quality biscuits served in with various sweets. My friends prefer those biscuits in our house to the formally prepared Engera and Tsebhis. To the fact, I used to be selective on picking different and exceptional sweets while visiting every house, we still do, chocolate ones are more preferred than normal or local candies.

Beyond all of these stuffs the day allows the people to share a moment of love and joy and on the way it becomes a means to strengthen the unity of all families, friends; near and far, co-workers, new guests do get introduced while visiting homes to chat over matters hence they develop worthy networks afterwards. It is a moment where people get over their quarrels and angriness and misunderstandings to deliver a sense of peace between themselves and their partners.

It is a moment where all people in the world build their relations and connections through many ways, thanks to Alexander Graham Bell who brought us the telephone, that is another way we can connect with each other. Anyone who has witnessed and above all shared the times of Eid in our country would definitely understand it how precious the moments are. It provides one a sense of lasting joy and it has indescribable feelings when friends and families gather in one of the member's house to share the day with the stunning smell of coffee, the Himbasha (homemade sweet bread), the cakes, the chit chats alongside the endless laughter, where the honorable guests applaud and wish the household the same time next year by saying in local tone as: Entay mo Tumat Nerkum... Ni Ameta Kemzi Ewan Trah.

Everyone develops such harmonious and joyful events to be part of their festivities.

Ever since old times, this kind of sharing festivities among our fathers and forefathers has become a strong and long lasting positive culture commonly seen and shared between the Muslims and the Christians, and still is followed. I believe the Eid beholds Kier to all of us people and Eid Mubarek. Book yourself an Eid invitation not to miss the wonderful Eid Etiquettes. It is everywhere an Abshiru or a Welcome moment.

'Writing our history

Alemseged Tesfay in a sense is Eritra's Chinua Achebe, born in 1944 in Adi Quala, Alemseged is widely known for his Historical Narratives, Novels, Essays and Dramas. Heavily influenced by the fact that he couldn't find any Literature written by Eritreans in his studies abroad, Mr. Alemseged has in many ways than one, had dedicated his life to creating what he couldn't find in his younger years as a student, Eritrean Literature, written by Eritrean. Alemseged's most widely read book, Aynifelale, the first of what was going to be a three volume historical narrative of colonial Eritrea, a lifetime spent in perfecting a well-researched and documented History of Eritrea from 1941 to 1950- was first published in 2001. His first book, in my perspective, is rightly held as a modern Eritrean masterpiece. Alemseged in all his written master pieces showed, writing our history is a powerful tool in the fight to regain 'what is ours, the Eritrean Identity!

Alemseged's third volume, Eritrea; From Federation to Occupation and Revolution, after a long wait, was inaugurated this past Friday at the G3 hall at Expo Grounds in front of a pact audience, which I was lucky enough to attend. The ground might had been fully pact, but these were just a small portion of Alemseged Tesfai's avid fans, having waited eagerly for years for the piece to be finished and presented, the look on most faces of the attendees said it all, they were proud.

Alemseged Tesfai leaves in his books a powerful legacy; a literary titan, who is at the forefront of Eritrean literature on his ongoing career and who is the author of the most widely read Eritrea book in history. He is a man trying to define his identity and his nations'.

A life time spent writing Eritrean literature, their positive impact on individuals, society and the nation; has hit its epitome; as Alemseged Tesfai's books published over the years have encouraged hopeful writers to take the path towards being published writers, if not all, most of this unprecedented success is credit to prominent writers such as Alemseged Tesfai. Not only this but the culture of reading cultivated with such increasing number of writers coming to the fold of the publishing scene is also tribute to numerous

Eritrean books published over the course of Eritrean independence.

What we fail to give due appreciation is the effect reading has in nation building. The fact that reading broadens our perspective and, hence, can enable us find solutions for problems improving our productivity in any endeavor we undertake is a much discussed assertion. Productivity and development are some of the pillars of an effective nation building process. Indeed, economy is an important factor that greatly influences the progress of nation building.

In the past, reading was a hunting ground for priests and sheiks. They read for divine inspiration, for refuting heretic dogmas and in order to appease the Creator.

Not able to read, the masses listened and obeyed. Books were sacred because wiring itself was a divine gift bestowed on those who served the deity. Then came along Gutenberg with his movable printing machine! Priests and sheiks lost the readership monopoly. The clergy were not happy with the new invention. So they told their flock not to read this book and not to print that treatise, etc.

With the industrial revolution, books were mass produced. The clergy had to concede defeat. Reading was open to the public. And to add insult to the injury (as far as the clergy were concerned) libraries were opened everywhere. Writing and reading which had before a divine origin lost their mystique and became accessible to profane hands and eyes.

It is said that at some point in history we Eritreans were not a reading people. We prefer to see and listen. This means that we liked the radio and television more than reading books or the newspaper. One obvious reason for this can be illiteracy. But even those who could read not only in their own language but in those of other languages were not much given to reading.

Don't read, talk! Was what their friends said to them in a café or a snack bar. They wanted them to be with them physically and spiritually. If someone is reading, that person is in the clouds, and it is the duty of friends to bring him/her down to the ground.

I know a bibliophile (One who hates books) when I see one. Once I lent an acquaintance a book for a week.

"Are you enjoying the book?" I asked him on the phone.

"Yes. Thank you. I am on page 101, and I will give you when I finish it," he said.

A genuine reader wouldn't say that. He was simply faking it.

Some could not fake it for a long time. They implode through excess of snobbism.

"Which is the most interesting book that you have read in your life?"

"Certainly, it is the Asmara's Telephone Directory,"

But reading is a habit. It becomes second nature. There are people who grow up reading books and when they are left alone without a book to fix their eyes on, they literally panic. For such people, there are cheap books on sale at railways stations in Europe. Just buy a 1 dollar fiction, open it when the train begins to move, and toss it at the next station.

On our culture though, it is very rare to see bus passengers reading during their commute. Few people are seen reading in the doctor's waiting room. I do wish they had good books or magazines in such places.

How about libraries? Before independence, according to one librarian, most of the readers who visited public libraries were jobless people, and some were eventual mental cases. The sane of mind were not regular 'clients' according to the librarian.

On the other hand, during the struggle days reading became a kind of culture in the field among combatants. Imagine writing and reading in your own language and in your own culture. Prices were awarded for best writers and translators in the field and as a result the habit or reading caught on and everywhere behind enemy lines and in various tranches the fighters kept on reading. Scholars such as Alemseged Tesfai's, who abandoned their studies abroad and joined the struggle played a prominent role in the struggle's own struggle to nurture and keep intact the Eritrean culture and history. Alemseged Tesfai in his infinite capacity, wrote and directed plays, whilst finding the time to write about the struggle, the very people that kept it striving. Literary works such as Wedi Hadera, Libi Tegadalay (Heart of a Fighter), Fetawi Seat, From Badme to Sahel, Etti kali'e Kunat (The Other War), were all written during the armed struggle. Alemseged encouraged his students and actors and actresses to develop the habit of reading during war time, and so did his prodigies. There is a big lesson to be learned for the lazybones here, namely that one doesn't need a sofa to be able to read. The avid reader can read between battles and within canon's range!

There are combatants who left for the field with little formal education and who at present can silence University professors in seconds. And there are those who had obtained their degree thirty or forty years back from such and such university and have never since read a single book to improve themselves. While the former deserve a university degree for the efforts they made, the latter should be despoiled of their academic honors for allowing darkness to envelop their minds.

Again I say that reading is a habit and should be learned quite young. Here, the parents have a very big responsibility. A child who grows up without consecrating a few hours for reading at home soon develops aversion to books and will be heading towards the dark tunnel where eyes and hearts are blinded and conceited whisperings of self are interpreted as knowledge.

What is therefore the best way to develop the culture of reading in a given society?

In the first place, the parents should themselves become an example. They should buy bookshelves and show some respect to books. If for example a father is overheard by his children complaining about the price of a book while spending 3000 Nfa on a sheep, what do you think the children will think?

Next, the number of public libraries should increase yearly along with the formation of book clubs at school lever. There should be book reviews on newspapers and panel discussions in the radio and the TV.

Furthermore, people should take the initiative to write stories for children in simple language. The child can learn to appreciate books only if the subject interests him/her and if only the language is simple and readable.

When in New York the authorities discovered that most of the Ghetto people could not read or write, they introduced books that narrated about sex, crime and violence. The Ghetto boys liked the books, because they could relate to it. Within a short time, those who could not differentiate A from B became avid readers and they asked for more books and libraries.

That's how you make people learn to read and eventually to love books.

A while back I visited a friend, who thought books had other purposes than to be opened and read. To make matters worse, he lived with his otherwise illiterate mother. I had my dinner with the family and I was asked to spend the night, which I accepted.

"Do you have some interesting books to read for the night?" I asked preparing myself for any eventuality.

"I have some encyclopedia," he said.

"You like reading the encyclopedia," I asked.

"Well, you see, this one here I use to prop up or support the old family wardrobe," he said in a causal manner.

"What about this one? I inquired pointing to one lying on the bed.

"I use that one to bolster the pillow," he replied.

I saw another one under the bed, probably used as a footstool, but preferred to keep silent.

I'm sure his mother went one better and burned the whole set of Encyclopedia Britannica from A to Z to brew her coffee. It seems that in this way both mother and son got more light (and warmth) from the books by burning them than by reading them.

I looked around for a bookshelf, in vain. Probably burned with lofty treaties and learned dissertations.

My friend grew up hating books, for he was told to read books he little understood or that did not tune with his temperament. Before one reads for knowledge, one should read for curiosity and for entertainment.

Social Gathering

The Eritrean people are highly inclined and are very fond of social gatherings of any kind which bring people together. I say this not because I am an Eritrean, but I know for a fact that they really look for occasions to be together, work together, celebrate, laugh, cry and face hardships together.

The people's aptitude to set schedules and create events whereby young and old come together, is just beyond belief. That is maybe why every cultural or agricultural undertaking is traditionally bound to have a rite for accompaniment. When, at present days, we vigorously see or experience the notion of what I choose to call 'Eritrean togetherness' it's actually nothing new, it has been there for hundreds of years.

Very recently, the inhabitants of Asmara celebrated the veneration of Saint Mary, Saint Michael, in addition to the celebration of the rest of the saints over the course of a year and how essentially their veneration is related to the notion and essence of coming together.

The Orthodox religion has been around for long, it has apportioned its branches to several cultural activities emulating established traits. The veneration of saints could be a major example. Conventionally, the Tewahdo Orthodox Church in Eritrea has a calendar whereby days of a month are subdivided in working days and holidays: the holidays are each reserved for saints accordingly. Of course it would be impractical to celebrate every saint's 'holyday' nationwide, but it is very practical and standard to observe their yearly anniversary at neighborhood or village level.

The technical approach to this celebration is beautiful. It works as follows: every neighborhood, every village and town has a church acclaimed to a specific saint, hence, the churches are somehow also emblems of neighborhoods and villages. Commonly, if one asks you about your neighborhood and you mention the name of the saint given to your neighborhood's church, then, there is no need for you to give out the street number of your address, it is actually easier that way, and much comfortable for older people who prefer to memorize the names of saints rather than street names or numbers!

People also use churches as referral points when giving out directions or even for meeting locations. And when it is actually time for the yearly anniversary of a saint, then the neighborhood, which houses the church, claimed after a certain saint, has the duty of observing the festivity. In Tigrigna, such festivities are called Nigdet.

Last week, on the 21st of November, the Saint Michael Nigdet was observed, while the 30th of November was the day of Saint Mary, two of the most venerated saints nationwide. In Asmara, the biggest church is the Saint Mary Church followed by that of Saint Michael. The neighborhoods of Asmara and towns around the country, which celebrate these days are multiple in number.

An ordinary Nigdet day would start by an early morning coffee ceremony at household level aimed at giving thanks to a saint, this is a must, even if it's not your neighborhood's Nigdet. The elders go to church as early as possible while youngsters are obliged to set out a candle light coffee ceremony in the kitchen added by a delightful breakfast. It all happens so early, that all of this, is executed before 8 o'clock: time for work or school. While if your neighborhood is hosting the Nigdet then the day starts even earlier. Families spend days in preparing food and drinks for pilgrims.

Once again and beautifully as ever, this is not a practice reserved only to Orthodox followers or Christians at large; similarly to all customs and habits in Eritrea, there is no discrimination. Muslim families and friends might not venerate Christian saints but certainly celebrate equally at a family member's, friends' or neighbor's house. Our mothers help each other in cooking the food, our fathers shop together and, we, youngsters will do very well lusciously munch for lunch and dinner together!

A neighborhood, village or town hosting Nigdet would normally get extremely crowded. Nigdets are national events of the people that see increased traveling circulations from a neighbor to another, a village to a village, town to town and city to another. Churches start mass prayer at midnight and with the high flow of faithful the covenant is put in the church's yard, or outside sometimes –by the way, it is a sight not to miss, the spiritual rites devoted to the saint I mean, so beautiful and so colorful. Shops are the busiest as well as local businesses. Consequently, public service is in the same way provided to ease the swarming flow of people moving around; more public transportation services and security patrols are put in place.

Lunch time is the most hectic episode of the day, friends and family from all walks of life gather for lunch, shame on you if you close the door!

So what happens is that when it's actually a neighborhood's Nigdet; families leave the doors to their houses open for family, friends and strangers to stop by for a meal. And as the doors are open, one is just welcome to go in and enjoy the delicacies prepared by the hosting family. The meal is free, drinks and coffee too, it's all gratis!

The pilgrims do their best to schedule their free time accordingly, one can't just leave any family or friend's house out. So we go systematically to avoid a nutrition overdose; mental framework for the schedule for a Nigdet day goes like: "Auntie X cooks meat medium rare so my first step is her house, my uncle's wife Y has the best seasoning of veggies so definitely going there for second plate, my friend's mom Z possesses magical desserts coming out of her oven so for sure I'll set my sweet tooth at my friend's... oh and can't dare to leave out my teacher's ginger-licious coffee!"

That's how it goes, really.

Nigdets are not only about food though, they have physiological impacts that overpass the superficial gathering we perceive at eye sight. They are actually some sort of health therapy structures of the Eritrean community. Doesn't the principle of health incorporate social, physical, emotional, mental and spiritual wellbeing? I think so... therefore, I believe that Nigdets are healthy practices.

How so? Well, first of all, for the sake of Nigdets people gather from all corners of the country, some sort of cross towns and cross cities excursions no matter the distance. A great reason to travel and explore new places, definitely a cross cultural integration.

Going to families' and friends' house to ask about how they're doing and simply offer willingness and readiness to be at their assistance at any time, while renewing that pact of family hood without having to read vows out loud, and you know, just the assertion of being there for one another.

The physical healing comes in smiling the whole day welcoming people, but let's lubricate the word people, to brothers and sisters, because that is how it actually feels. And one more adorable thing about Nigdet, is that it never comes as a burden to the hosting family in terms of energy, for the reason that the children's' cousins and friends have the deliberate duty of spending a couple of nights to actually help with cooking, cleaning and the endless domestic works.

Marvelously, it is also an emotional and mental rectifying occasions as people come together, children make new friends and cousins that they'd only would hear of year long. Also, families feel some sort of tranquility in sending a helping hand when they deliver food and beverage to the church in the morning. After the churches' celebrations are over and the covenant is put back to its place, the clergy takes on the mission of distributing food to the less fortunate.

And how is Nigdet spiritually befitting? Well, there is a great difference between praying alone and together, anyone that knows would not deny. After all, I believe that is exactly why people gather in mosques and churches: to feel solidarity in imploring love and peace for a communal wellbeing. Mass prayers during such occasions start at midnight and last until midday and past it at times.

And for such reasons and more, Nigdets, the veneration of saints and their cultural practices, uphold amazing values of unity, integrity, accord and harmony.

Years go by and generation pass as well, and new global conventions might conceal the traditional ones, but then again I guess, practices like these ones make globalization weak in penetrating and positioning as conventional. Seeing how Eritreans love to come together and will engineer just about anything to actually make it happen, it will definitely be a though wall to break through!

Homage to coffee: A colorful nature of Eritrean culture

The scent of ground coffee and refreshing aroma of hissing espresso machines is a welcoming nature of the downtown streets of Asmara and other towns in Eritrea. Almost every café in most cities of the country, especially the capital Asmara, happens to own magnificent models of espresso machines and wonderful people who operate them. It is a common tradition in Asmara asking friends for a cup of espresso or macchiato; usually the one who asks takes the bill. But inviting someone for a coffee at your place is a profound tradition in every part of Eritrea.

Coffee is a traditional brew in most ethnic groups of Eritrea, each of which possesses variety of ways in preparing the coffee ceremony. Taking the Tigrinya culture for instance, coffee is prepared as a gesture of warm hospitality especially for guests who come a long way. However, drinking coffee in Eritrea is not just about pouring a concentrated coffee beverage into a cup or whatever sort of chinaware is used for that purpose.

Preparing coffee, or maybe we should call it a coffee ceremony in this case, would take more than an hour starting from the very beginning of roasting the coffee beans to serving the final brew of the coffee. For this reason, preparing coffee for someone in Eritrea would mean that you are going to have a long and nice chat with that person.

A wife often waits hours for her husband to arrive form work or any place he might have gone to, so that they could drink coffee together. In fact, it is most common at that moment that Eritrean couple gets to have quality time together, talk about things and catch-up with each other. Indeed, that would be the perfect moment for the couple to create a cozy atmosphere to talk their hearts out.

Traditionally, coffee in most parts of Eritrea is prepared by putting ground coffee in a coffee pot, usually made of clay. But first the coffee beans should be roasted and grinded. Then you mix the ground coffee with water, which of course the proportion differs determining the strength of the coffee. Later, heat is applied to the brew until the beverage tends to burst out of the top of the clay pot.

In most occasions, coffee in Eritrea is served three times for each guest. The first cup is obviously the best as the coffee-water proportion in the brew is normally coffee dominant and is by far very strong. Hence the following two or three rounds get diluent and weaker as the water takes over the proportion.

Aboy Goitom is an 80 year old man who worked for a little more than 55 years as a 'Gaggia', an old espresso machine, operator at one of Asmara's oldest bars in the downtown streets. The old man said, "I know the machine like the back of my hand, besides we have more than half a century connection", but he bluntly admitted that the coffee he has at home with his family is unparalleled. Aboy Goitom said, "The coffee in the cafes, like in most international ways is brewed by forcing very hot steaming water under high pressure through ground coffee. And the coffee is best served hot. That is normally called, as adopted from the Italian language, espresso."

While explaining on how the coffee is prepared at home however, Aboy Goitom said, " First my wife roasts the coffee until they become oily brown, lesser than a dark brown if you want to have a tasty coffee, and makes me smell the smoldering coffee beans from the 'Menkeshkesh', a custom made metal pan especially made for roasting the coffee. Then the ground coffee powder is added to a pot, usually made of clay, Jebena, and is mixed with water. Then you put the Jebena on a burning coal to boil, where the aroma of boiling coffee smells from a distance. In the process, the coffee has to burst forth from the pot three times, and every time the women performing the ceremony put the coffee burst from the pot in another cup and return it to the pot after the pot cools off for some time, this is done three times, and after the coffee is boiled properly they put down the Jebena, for a couple of minutes and is ready to serve."

"As far as I know in my own culture which is Tigrinia" ,Aboy Goitom said, "Along with the coffee ceremony it is very common to see popcorn served and Frankincense burned for good scent, and coffee is drunk in a small cup, Fenjal. Coffee is drunk in three rounds, four in some cases, but no additional beans are roasted, the women will put some water and coffee powder left for this purpose and make it boil for the second and the third rounds. The first round is called as "Awol", the second "Kalayieti" and the third is "Bereka" if they serve the fourth, usually if you want to maintain the mood, they call it "Dereja". Customarily one has to attend until the third round, and once all the three rounds are over, the guests bless the house of the host and the women who performed the ceremony."

Normally, coffee ceremony in Eritrea is an integral part of the social and cultural life. An invitation to attend a coffee ceremony is considered an insignia of friendship or respect and is an excellent example of Eritrean hospitality, among others. Performing the ceremony is almost obligatory in the presence of guests from distant places, whatever time the guests may come. You should not be in a hurry though, because this special ceremony can take a few hours. So you have to sit back and enjoy, because it is most definitely one of the times you get your nerves relaxed.

For an ordinary or maybe a typical family in the Tigrinya ethnicity, it is the women's duty to prepare the coffee and the men normally appreciate and comment on the quality of the brew. Nonetheless, in other ethnic groups in Eritrea, such as Tigre and Hedareb, the men, mostly herdsmen, carry all the gears they need, such as a metal "Jebena" and raw coffee beans so as to make coffee in every place they sit to take a rest and graze their herds.

Eritrea's homage to coffee is sometimes elaborate, and always beautifully ceremonial. The tradition in preparing coffee has not changed its taste for centuries and occupies a center stage in the country's value of culture, which portrays the true hospitable nature of Eritreans.

Tour, See and Believe!

Generally speaking, people tend to fail to appreciate what is proximate and within their hands. A traditional Eritrean saying states, "ab edka zelo werqs darga cherqi," which roughly translates as: "anybody feels not a precious thing they own but take it as cheap."

It is quite impressive to look at wealthy nations' developments and infrastructural advances. The skyscrapers, stylish and imposing real estate, and huge human-made landmarks get all our attention. But that doesn't belong to us. What is ours is found not far away, and only needs us to pay a visit. It is not just the cities or main towns that hold the beauty of a country; often, the most fascinating subjects lay outside their boundaries. So every once in a one while, one needs to take a journey to visit some of these, at times, overlooked sites that are relatively near when compared to the attractions miles away.

All of this reminds me of the lyrics of an old song which goes "Zuro mo Hagerga Temt Teazeba

Habtam Ztefetro Adi Wehayz Ruba... Bealti Akranat Abeyti Taba..." The song simply reflects on the beauty of local Eritrean landmarks and culture and encourages listeners to visit all of the country's territory. Seemingly following its suggestions, I did visit some of the unique and attractive places in the country.

Without overstating, I have been to some of the most remote areas of the country, except the Southern Red Sea region (which I hope to see in the future). I have been as far as Sawa in the Gash Barka region and also visited the Anseba region, which was on my way there. I have also managed to visit some parts of the Debub as well as the Northern Red Sea region. Within the Maekel region, a useful departing point, the major cities, towns, and roadways make me feel like the song has delivered its message. Locals should take every opportunity to explore their country, be it with family, colleagues, friends, or as an educational trip. Wherever the destination is, there are often an array of attractions, as well as interesting things along the way that are sure to capture the attentions and interests of travelers.

The long, winding road to the Fil-Fil Solomuna rainforest is, in itself, a mesmerizing infrastructural feat. One cannot help but admire how gorgeously constructed the road is before actually reaching the final green zone. Moreover, historical and archeological sites can be found within different parts of the country, and their appearance within the background is a stunning reminder of the inherent beauty and treasures of the nation.

Recently, I had the opportunity to attend a tour organized by the May Mslam Dam (or commonly referred to as the Gergera Dam). It is massive, appears well-built, and is part of the national strategy and policy of sustainable development. Based on information gathered from sources at the dam site (including the engineer and project manager), the May Mslam Dam is one of the largest projects undertaken by the Government of Eritrea, representing a considerable investment toward socio-economic growth and sustainable development. An engineer at the site noted that approximately half a billion Nakfa was extended towards the completion of the dam, the construction of which began in mid-2011 and finalized by 2014. Some irregularities in the construction were discovered in between due to a shortage of supplies and labor; however, only after two years from its formal beginning, the majority of the task (approximately 75%) was done in about only 6 months. The dam has a 35 meter diameter, with a 7 meter depth and stands 38 constructed above the ground.

The foundation raised above consists of approximately a 6 meter diameter and is stretched nearly 750 meters long.

Four rivers feed the dam: from Guh Chea, from the Tslma villages, from Adi Halo, and from around the

Emba Teqera area. Collectively, these cover an area of 431 sq. km until the last point of the dam, but overall the dam covers 3.7sq.km, and currently holds around 33 million mm cubed of water and can reach up to 50 million mm cubed. In addition to the rivers, the dam can hold significant supplies of rainwater (extending up to approximately three years).

Segen Construction Company provided the technical management, design and supply for the dam, and was joined in construction by military forces, students, and citizens engaged in community-development summer programs from all over the nation. Importantly, the dam serves to reflect how Eritreans, from all walks of life, have been engaged in promoting development and working to tangibly improve the standard of life across the country.

The main aim of the dam is to support the surrounding agricultural areas and improve the livelihoods of people living in the neighboring towns. Currently, a pilot project is in progress within the Halhale and Tslma agricultural fields, using water supplied directly from the dam. As well, the dam will help contribute to people's daily lives by supplying clean water for the towns of Dekemhare, Dubarwa, Mendefera and other small towns.

Importantly, the dam and my visit in connection with International Tourism Day underscore that people (citizens in particular) should take the time to visit and explore a range of sites. For locals, visiting developmental sites can help familiarize them with the ongoing progress and realities of their nation, as well provide a glimpse of the future. It is important to also note that many other significant infrastructure and development projects are underway around the country, focused on improving socio-economic growth, while encouraging social inclusion and tangible, sustainable development. My advice? Go explore the really fascinating sites...tour, see, and believe!

www.ingramcontent.com/pod-product-compliance
Lightning Source LLC
Chambersburg PA
CBHW031107080526
44587CB00011B/866